101 BEST SUPER FOODS

Betsy A. Hornick, MS, RD

Publications International, Ltd.

Betsy A. Hornick, M.S., R.D., is a registered dietitian specializing in nutrition education and communications. She has written and edited numerous nutrition and health education publications for both consumers and health professionals, including materials published by the American Dietetic Association. She is co-author of The Healthy Beef Cookbook and a regular contributor to Diabetic Cooking magazine.

Recipes pictured on the front cover: Blueberry Soy Shake *(page 35)* and Roast Salmon with New Potatoes and Red Onions *(page 155).*

Recipe pictured on the back cover: Roasted Chili Turkey Breast with Cilantro-Lime Rice *(page 103).*

Photo Credits
Front Cover: PIL Collection (left and right); Shutterstock (center).

Back Cover: PIL Collection (bottom); Shutterstock (top)

Interior Art: Dreamstime, Photos to Go, PIL Collection, Shutterstock and Thinkstock.

ISBN-13: 978-1-4508-2268-8
ISBN-10: 1-4508-2268-1

Library of Congress Control Number: 1728700.

Manufactured in China.

8 7 6 5 4 3 2 1

Nutritional Analysis: Every effort has been made to check the accuracy of the nutritional information that appears with each recipe. However, because numerous variables account for a wide range of values for certain foods, nutritive analyses in this book should be considered approximate. Different results may be obtained by using different nutrient databases and different brand-name products.

Microwave Cooking: Microwave ovens vary in wattage. Use the cooking times as guidelines and check for doneness before adding more time.

Note: This book is for informational purposes Note: This publication is only intended to provide general information. The information is specifically not intended to be a substitute for medical diagnosis or treatment by your physician or other health care professional. You should always consult your own physician or other health care professionals about any medical questions, diagnosis, or treatment. (Products vary among manufacturers. Please check labels carefully to confirm nutritional values.)

The information obtained by you from this book should not be relied upon for any personal, nutritional, or medical decision. You should consult an appropriate professional for specific advice tailored to your specific situation. PIL makes no representations or warranties, express or implied, with respect to your use of this information.

In no event shall PIL, its affiliates or advertisers be liable for any direct, indirect, punitive, incidental, special, or consequential damages, or any damages whatsoever including, without limitation, damages for personal injury, death, damage to property, or loss of profits, arising out of or in any way connected with the use of any of the above-referenced information or otherwise arising out of the use of this book.

Publications International, Ltd.

Include Better Health on your Menu

Forget about denial. Today's approach to healthier eating is more about what to include in your daily menu and less about what to avoid. In fact, the government's latest Dietary Guidelines for Americans emphasize getting more fruits and vegetables, whole grains, low-fat and fat-free milk products, healthy fats and seafood. These are the types of nutrient-rich foods that have been linked to improved health and less disease—they're the "super foods."

That's not to say other foods can't fit in a healthful diet. But by eating more super foods, you'll naturally have less room for foods that offer little beyond calories. And before you know it, both your diet and your health will have improved. Introducing you to the wide variety, tempting flavors and amazing benefits of many of the super foods out there is what 101 *Best Super Foods* is all about.

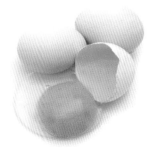

What Makes a Super Food Super?

Super foods are typically minimally processed, or whole foods, so they retain more of the balanced combination of nutrients nature gave them. These nutrients often include some mix of the essentials—the fiber, protein, vitamins, minerals and other familiar nutrients our bodies require to function properly and maintain good health. But they frequently also include various natural plant substances called phytonutrients that, according to a growing body of evidence, may play important roles in reducing the risk of ailments such as heart disease, high blood pressure, diabetes and cancer. Scientists are just beginning to identify these intriguing substances and learn how they, alone or in combination with each other and with essential nutrients, defend against disease. And the only way to capture the combined benefits and healing potential of all of these nutrients is to consume a wide variety of whole foods.

The super foods profiled in this book are a great place to start. Each profile introduces you to the potential health benefits of a different super food, includes instructions for choosing and storing the food, and provides healthy preparation and serving tips. Most profiles also include a delicious, healthy recipe.

To get the most from the foods in this book, however, keep these important instructions in mind:

1. Aim high when it comes to variety.

The 101 foods featured in this book have some remarkable qualities and potential benefits, but don't limit yourself. Enjoy them, but also use them as stepping stones to explore the many other healthy whole foods out there. Nutrient information per serving is provided for each food to help you make comparisons.

2. Select and store foods wisely.

Use the profiles to learn how to choose the freshest and healthiest varieties of the foods featured in this book. You'll be more likely to get the most nutrients and enjoyment from them. Likewise, follow the storage instructions given to help ensure the quality and safety of the foods on your plate.

3. Use smart preparation strategies.

To help ensure the foods you choose retain their health-enhancing character, get familiar with the preparation tips and strategies in the profiles. After all, even good-for-you foods can take a turn for the worse if you overcook them, strip them of nutrients or slather them with unnecessary coatings or sauces that pile on calories, unhealthy fats or loads of sodium.

4. Be adventurous.

Do your health a favor and try profiled foods that you've never tasted before (or perhaps tasted only as a child or only prepared one way) using recipes, such as those offered here, that bring out the best qualities of foods. Nutrients per serving are provided for each recipe to help you fit these foods in your overall diet.

Discovering—and taking advantage of—the health-enhancing potential of super foods may be one of the best steps you can take toward improving and protecting your health. Enjoy!

Acorn Squash

During fall and winter months, this winter squash—shaped a bit like a giant acorn—is in season and at its delicious best. With its sunny golden color and sweet-tasting flesh, acorn squash is a breeze to prepare yet packed with nutrients.

nutrients per serving:

Acorn Squash
¹/₂ cup cooked

Calories 57
Protein 1g
Total Fat 0g
Saturated Fat 0g
Cholesterol 0mg
Carbohydrate 15g
Dietary Fiber 4.5g
Sodium 0mg
Potassium 450mg
Calcium 45mg
Iron 0.9mg
Vitamin A 439 IU
Vitamin C 11mg
Folate 19mcg

benefits

Acorn squash is rich in vitamins A and C, folate and vitamin B_6. It also provides an array of phytonutrients, natural substances that can rid the body of toxins and may help prevent cancer. Acorn squash is also a good source of potassium, an important mineral for controlling blood pressure. And its high fiber content makes acorn squash satisfying and good for digestive health.

selection and storage

Although often available year-round, acorn squash is best from early fall to late winter. Look for acorn squash that is deeply colored (dark green with some golden coloring) and free of spots, bruises and mold. With its hard skin serving as a barrier, this winter squash can be stored a month or more in a dark, cool place.

preparation and serving tips

You can bake, steam, sauté or simmer acorn squash. For an easy way to add flavor and flair, try this trick: Cut a squash in half, scoop out the seeds, and bake about 45 minutes, then fill the center with whatever you like (try rice or couscous). Or simply scoop out the baked flesh, mash it and sprinkle with Parmesan cheese. Acorn squash also makes a tasty addition to savory soups.

couscous-stuffed squash

- 2 small acorn squash, halved lengthwise and seeded
- 1 medium poblano pepper, sliced
- 1 small onion, sliced
- 1¼ cups vegetable broth
- ½ cup shiitake mushrooms, chopped
- ¾ cup uncooked couscous
- 1 medium plum tomato, diced
- 2 tablespoons pine nuts

1. Preheat oven to 400°F. Spray baking sheet with nonstick cooking spray; place squash, cut side down, on baking sheet. Spread pepper and onion on baking sheet. Cover with foil; bake 35 to 40 minutes or until squash is tender.

2. Bring broth and mushrooms to a boil in medium saucepan over medium-high heat. Stir in couscous, tomato and pine nuts; cover and remove from heat. Let stand 5 minutes. Meanwhile, dice roasted pepper and onion; add to couscous mixture, fluffing couscous lightly with fork.

3. Turn squash cut side up. Fill each with ¾ cup couscous mixture. *Makes 4 servings*

Tip: Acorn squash have thick, hard skins that can be difficult to cut. To make cutting easier, soften them in the microwave. Pierce the skin with a fork; microwave on HIGH 1 to 2 minutes. Allow to cool for a few minutes, then slice lengthwise and remove the seeds.

nutrients per serving:

Calories 290	**Total Fat** 4g
Calories from Fat 12%	**Saturated Fat** <1g
Protein 9g	**Cholesterol** 0mg
Carbohydrate 57g	**Sodium** 187mg
Fiber 6g	

Almonds

Almonds are the flavorful, nutrient-rich seeds from the fruit of the almond tree. Versatile almonds are delicious additions to both sweet and savory dishes and are also made into almond butter and almond flour.

benefits

Almonds are little nutrient powerhouses. Ounce for ounce, they're one of the most nutrient dense tree nuts. Their protein, fiber and healthy monounsaturated fats provide lasting energy, benefit heart health and overall wellness, and even help reduce cancer risk. Almonds are also a good source of vitamin E and magnesium and provide calcium and B vitamins, as well. As with all nuts, however, calories can add up quickly, so watch your portions.

selection and storage

Almonds are available packaged or in bulk, with or without shells. Always check the freshness date on packaged almonds. If you buy bulk almonds, they should smell fresh. Packaged almonds are available in various forms— whole, blanched (to remove the skin), sliced, slivered, raw, dry or oil roasted, smoked, flavored and salted or unsalted. Almonds in the shell can keep for a few months in a cool, dry location. Once you shell them or open a package of shelled nuts, refrigerate or freeze them if you don't use them right away.

preparation and serving tips

Using almonds as a topping or in baking allows you to benefit from their nutrients without overdoing calories. As a snack, stick with a handful, or about 23 almonds (1 ounce). Toasting almonds in the oven or on the stove top intensifies their flavor. Enjoy almonds sprinkled on salads, soups, casseroles, vegetables, stir-fries, cereal and more.

nutrients per serving:

Almonds, dry roasted without salt 1 ounce

Calories 169
Protein 6g
Total Fat 15g
Saturated Fat 1g
Cholesterol 0mg
Carbohydrate 6g
Dietary Fiber 3g
Sodium 0mg
Potassium 200mg
Calcium 76mg
Iron 1mg
Folate 15mcg
Vitamin E 7mg
Magnesium 80mg

lemon almond biscotti

⅓ cup margarine, softened
⅔ cup granulated sugar
2 tablespoons grated lemon peel
1 teaspoon baking powder
½ teaspoon baking soda
⅛ teaspoon salt
2 eggs
2½ cups all-purpose flour
½ cup slivered almonds

1. Preheat oven to 375°F. Beat margarine in large bowl with electric mixer at medium speed 30 seconds. Add sugar, lemon peel, baking powder, baking soda and salt; beat until well blended. Beat in eggs. Add flour; beat until crumbly. (Dough will be fairly dry.) Stir in almonds.

2. Shape dough into two 9-inch logs. Flatten logs to 1½-inch thickness. Place on nonstick cookie sheet.

3. Bake 20 minutes or until toothpick inserted into centers of logs comes out clean. Cool on cookie sheet 1 hour.

4. Cut each log crosswise into 16 (½-inch) slices. Place slices cut side down on cookie sheet; bake 8 minutes. Turn and bake 8 minutes or until crisp and golden. Cool completely on wire racks. Store in airtight container.   *Makes 32 cookies*

nutrients per serving:

Calories 85
Calories from Fat 35%
Protein 2g
Carbohydrate 12g
Fiber <1g
Total Fat 3g
Saturated Fat <1g
Cholesterol 13mg
Sodium 70mg

Apples

There are thousands of apple varieties to choose from, so don't limit yourself to one or two. Whether you prefer tart or sweet, extra crunchy or soft and juicy, apples make great low-fat, high-fiber snacks and super desserts.

nutrients per serving:

**Apple
1 medium**

Calories 95
Protein <1g
Total Fat 0g
Saturated Fat 0g
Cholesterol 0g
Carbohydrate 25g
Dietary Fiber 4g
Sodium 0mg
Potassium 195mg
Calcium 11mg
Iron 0.2mg
Vitamin A 98 IU
Vitamin C 8mg
Folate 5mcg

benefits

Having a spot in our hearts—and diets—for apples may pay off in better heart health. While they're not bursting with nutrients, apples provide vitamin C, an antioxidant that may help prevent heart disease and some cancers. And their soluble fiber may help keep blood cholesterol levels in check. Regularly snacking on apples may even help keep a healthy smile on your face by stimulating your gums.

selection and storage

Although a few varieties— Golden Delicious, Jonathan and Winesap, for example— are considered all-purpose, you're generally best off choosing apples based on their intended uses. For baking, try Empire, Rome Beauty, Cortland, Northern Spy or Ida Red; they deliver flavor and keep their shape when cooked. For eating raw, you can't beat Gala, Fuji, Braeburn or Honeycrisp. Apples prefer humid air, so the crisper drawer of the refrigerator is the best place to store them. Some varieties will keep for several months, though most get mealy in a month or two.

preparation and serving tips

Supermarket apples are often waxed, which can seal in pesticide residues on the skin. And even apples you pick yourself may have been exposed to contaminants. So always wash your apples. (You could peel them, but that removes a lot of beneficial fiber.) To keep apples from browning when cut, sprinkle a little lemon juice on cut surfaces.

apple & carrot casserole

- 6 large carrots, sliced
- 4 large apples, peeled, cored and sliced
- ¼ cup plus 1 tablespoon all-purpose flour
- 1 tablespoon brown sugar
- ½ teaspoon ground nutmeg
- 1 tablespoon butter
- ½ cup orange juice
- ½ teaspoon salt (optional)

1. Preheat oven to 350°F. Cook carrots in boiling water in large saucepan 5 minutes; drain. Layer carrots and apples in large casserole.

2. Combine flour, brown sugar and nutmeg in small bowl; sprinkle over top. Dot with butter. Pour orange juice over casserole. Sprinkle with salt, if desired. Bake 30 minutes or until carrots are tender.

Makes 6 servings

Apricots

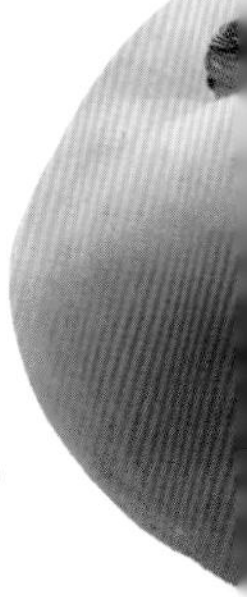

For such diminutive, delicate fruit, apricots are a surprisingly robust source of fiber, beta-carotene, iron and potassium. Their fragrant aroma and sweet taste make fresh apricots delightful for dessert or as a snack.

nutrients per serving:

Apricot
1 medium

Calories 17
Protein <1g
Total Fat 0g
Saturated Fat 0g
Cholesterol 0g
Carbohydrate 4g
Dietary Fiber 0.5g
Sodium 0mg
Potassium 90mg
Calcium 5mg
Iron 0.1mg
Vitamin A 764 IU
Vitamin C 4mg
Folate 3mcg

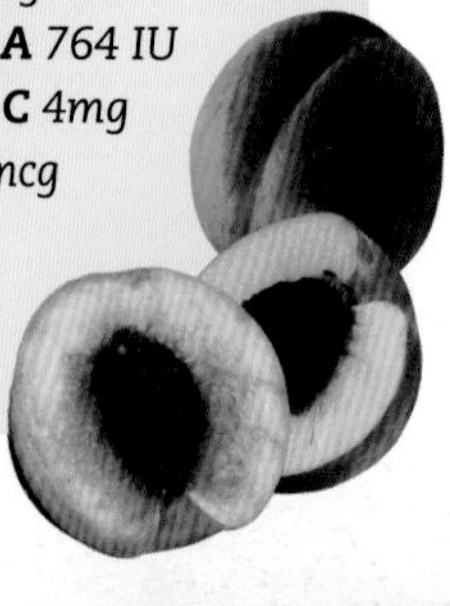

benefits

Apricots are abundant in soluble fiber, which helps lower blood cholesterol levels. But the real heart-related news about apricots is that they're brimming with vitamin A (beta-carotene), an important antioxidant that's linked to the prevention of certain cancers, cataracts and heart disease. And the potassium they provide helps maintain normal blood pressure. Be aware, though, that sugar is often added during commercial canning, and the high heat used in the process destroys some nutrients. The drying process, on the other hand, concentrates the nutrients—including the carbohydrates—so ½ cup of dried apricots yields three times the calories of a single serving of fresh.

selection and storage

Fresh apricots are fragile and must be handled with care. Look for plump, golden orange apricots that are fairly firm. You may need to ripen the fruit for a day or two at room temperature before you can enjoy them. But don't pile them up, because the pressure will cause them to bruise as they ripen. Once they are ripe, store them in the refrigerator. Since this fruit's season is short and sweet, canned and dried apricots offer delicious alternatives to fresh.

preparation and serving tips

Be gentle when washing fresh apricots. To reap the most health benefits, eat the skins and all. If you use canned apricots, rinse them before eating to wash away the sugar-rich syrup.

nutrients per serving:

Calories 175
Calories from Fat 21%
Protein 10g
Carbohydrate 26g
Fiber 3g

Total Fat 4g
Saturated Fat 1g
Cholesterol 17mg
Sodium 348mg

apricot chicken sandwiches

- 6 ounces poached or baked chicken tenders, diced
- 2 tablespoons chopped pitted fresh apricots
- 2 tablespoons no-sugar-added apricot fruit spread
- 4 slices whole wheat bread
- 4 lettuce leaves

1. Combine chicken, apricots and fruit spread in medium bowl.

2. Top two bread slices with lettuce. Top evenly with chicken mixture and remaining two bread slices. Cut sandwiches into quarters. *Makes 4 servings*

Artichokes

Protected by their spiky green leaves, artichokes look hard to handle at first. Once you learn some simple preparations, the delicate, buttery taste makes getting to know this high-fiber vegetable well worth it.

benefits

Low-calorie artichokes are rich in insoluble fiber (good for the digestive system) and potassium (beneficial to blood pressure). Artichokes are also a source of folate, a vitamin that's especially important for women in their childbearing years because it helps prevent birth defects. Research also links long-term deficiencies of folate to an increased risk of heart disease. Compared to the artichoke heart, the meaty leaves contain more nutrients.

selection and storage

Fresh artichokes are available in the produce department. (Baby artichokes are actually side growths of the plant.) Look for a soft green color and tightly packed, closed leaves. Store artichokes in a plastic bag in the refrigerator with a few drops of water to prevent them from drying out. Although best if used within a few days, they'll keep for a week or two if stored properly. Artichoke hearts, the vegetable's meaty base, are also available canned or marinated and jarred.

preparation and serving tips

Wash artichokes under running water. Pull off outer, lower leaves and trim the sharp tips from the outer leaves. Boil for 20 to 40 minutes or steam for 25 to 40 minutes or until a leaf pulls out easily. Artichokes can be served hot or cold, but instead of dipping the leaves in butter or hollandaise sauce, opt for lemon juice with a dash of olive oil.

nutrients per serving:

**Artichoke
1 medium cooked**

Calories 64
Protein 3g
Total Fat 0g
Saturated Fat 0g
Cholesterol 0g
Carbohydrate 14g
Dietary Fiber 10g
Sodium 70mg
Potassium 340mg
Calcium 25mg
Iron 0.7mg
Vitamin A 16 IU
Vitamin C 9mg
Folate 107mcg

tuna artichoke cups

1 can (6 ounces) tuna packed in
    water, preferably albacore,
    drained, liquid reserved
¼ cup minced shallots
1 tablespoon white wine vinegar
¼ teaspoon ground coriander
4 ounces cream cheese
1 can (14 ounces) artichoke hearts,
    drained and coarsely chopped
1 tablespoon lemon juice
½ teaspoon salt
¼ teaspoon white pepper
    Dash ground nutmeg
12 wonton wrappers
2 tablespoons unsalted butter,
    melted

1. Preheat oven to 350°F. Heat reserved tuna liquid, shallots, vinegar and coriander in small saucepan over medium-high heat. Bring to a boil. Reduce heat; simmer, uncovered, until liquid evaporates. Add tuna and cream cheese; cook, stirring constantly, until cheese melts. Stir in artichokes, lemon juice, salt, pepper and nutmeg. Cool slightly.

2. Gently press 1 wonton wrapper into 12 standard (2½-inch) muffin cups, allowing ends to extend above edges of cups. Spoon tuna mixture evenly into wonton wrappers.

3. Brush edges of wonton wrappers with melted butter. Bake 20 minutes or until tuna mixture is set and edges of wonton wrappers are browned.

Makes 12 appetizers

nutrients per serving:

Calories 100
Calories from Fat 50%
Protein 6g
Carbohydrate 7g
Fiber <1g
Total Fat 6g
Saturated Fat 3g
Cholesterol 21mg
Sodium 288mg

Arugula

One of the most nutritious of all salad greens, peppery, mustard-flavored arugula is a member of the same plant family as broccoli and cauliflower. Arugula's delicate, lacy leaves add zip to any salad or pasta.

benefits

Arugula has more calcium than most other salad greens and is a good source of vitamin C, beta-carotene, iron and folate. Reflecting its cruciferous-family roots, arugula is loaded with phytonutrients that have the antioxidant power to detoxify the body naturally. Recent research also suggests arugula may help relieve gastric ulcers.

selection and storage

Arugula is usually sold in small bunches. Look for leaves that are bright green and fresh looking. Arugula is very perishable and should be refrigerated, unwashed in a sealed bag, and used within a few days. You may also find baby arugula—younger, more tender leaves that are less spicy than the more mature greens. With the popularity of baby arugula growing, prewashed packages of these leaves are usually available in your grocer's refrigerated produce section. Prepackaged greens will cost more but save you the chore of washing away the gritty dirt that clings to the leaves.

preparation and serving tips

Arugula is a very social green, going well in mixed green salads, substituting for basil in pesto sauces and stepping in for spinach. Arugula is also attractive on its own, in a fresh salad with a simple olive oil and lemon juice dressing and a few shavings of Parmesan cheese. Arugula leaves are a lively addition to pasta dishes, soups and sautéed vegetables, too; add them right before serving so the leaves gently wilt.

nutrients per serving:

Arugula	**Saturated Fat** 0g	**Calcium** 32mg
1 cup	**Cholesterol** 0g	**Iron** 0.3mg
	Carbohydrate 1g	**Vitamin A** 475 IU
Calories 5	**Dietary Fiber** <1g	**Vitamin C** 3mg
Protein <1g	**Sodium** 5mg	**Folate** 19mcg
Total Fat 0g	**Potassium** 70mg	

Asparagus

Tall, slender asparagus is one of the first signs of spring, when it is plentiful, fresh and affordable. As a side dish or a delicious part of a stir-fry or casserole, it's hard to beat asparagus for flavor and nutrition.

benefits

Asparagus is a winner when it comes to folate, a vitamin that helps prevent neural-tube birth defects. It also provides potassium, an important mineral for blood pressure control. Two major antioxidants—beta-carotene and vitamin C—are abundant in asparagus and appear to play important roles in the fight against heart disease and cancer.

selection and storage

The first fresh asparagus arrives at farmers' markets in early spring. Look for bright green, smooth, firm and straight stalks. Tips should be compact, closed, pointed and purplish in color. Choose stalks of similar size so they'll cook at the same rate. Wrapped loosely in a plastic bag in the vegetable drawer, or placed upright in a glass or bowl with an inch of water in the refrigerator, the stalks will keep for almost a week. Fresh asparagus may be blanched, drained well and packed in freezer bags; use within eight months.

preparation and serving tips

Rinse the stalks thoroughly and snap off the whitish stem ends. Add the ends to soup stock instead of tossing them out. Boil, steam or microwave asparagus, but avoid overcooking it. You can also give it a light brushing of olive oil and grill or roast it. Cooked correctly, the spears should be crisp-tender and bright green. Overcooked spears turn mushy and a drab olive green. Serve asparagus hot, warm or cold. For a twist, add cut-up asparagus to your next stir-fry or pasta dish.

nutrients per serving:

Asparagus
½ cup cooked

Calories 20
Protein 2g
Total Fat 0g
Saturated Fat 0g
Cholesterol 0g
Carbohydrate 4g
Dietary Fiber 2g
Sodium 10mg
Potassium 200mg
Calcium 21mg
Iron 0.8mg
Vitamin A 905 IU
Vitamin C 7mg
Folate 134mcg

Avocado

You may only know this rich, smooth-textured fruit as the main ingredient in guacamole, but its buttery flavor also complements vegetable, meat, salad and pasta dishes.

benefits

Although rich in folate, vitamin A and potassium, this unique fruit is very high in calories, 85 percent of which come from fat. Fortunately for us, the fat is the heart-friendly monounsaturated variety, so it doesn't raise blood cholesterol levels. Avocado also contains lutein, an antioxidant that helps maintain healthy eyes and skin.

selection and storage

The two most common varieties of avocados are the pebbly-skinned, dark green Haas and the smoother-skinned, larger Florida avocado. Ripe avocados yield to gentle pressure and should be unblemished and heavy for their size. If you won't be using them right away, choose avocados that are firm. You can always speed ripening by placing them in a brown paper bag. Once ripened, avocados can be stored in the refrigerator for several days.

preparation and serving tips

Avocados should be served raw because they have a bitter taste when cooked. If you want to use them in a hot pasta or vegetable dish or with cooked meat or poultry, add them just before serving. Once avocado flesh is cut and exposed to air, it browns rapidly. Adding the avocado to a dish at the last minute helps minimize this, as does tossing the cut avocado with lemon or lime juice. Contrary to popular belief, burying the avocado pit in mashed avocado will not help the flesh maintain its color.

nutrients per serving:

Avocado
½ medium

Calories 161
Protein 2g
Total Fat 15g
Saturated Fat 2g
Cholesterol 0g

Carbohydrate 9g
Dietary Fiber 6.5g
Sodium 5mg
Potassium 485mg
Calcium 12mg
Iron 0.5mg
Vitamin A 147 IU
Vitamin C 10mg
Folate 81mcg

shrimp and avocado tostadas

1 cup canned low-fat refried black beans
  Nonstick cooking spray
8 ounces medium raw shrimp, peeled
3 cloves garlic, minced
3 green onions, thickly sliced
½ cup salsa
1 ripe avocado, diced
4 tostada shells, warmed
½ cup shredded romaine lettuce
½ cup diced tomato

1. Heat refried beans in small saucepan over medium heat.

2. Meanwhile, spray large nonstick skillet with cooking spray and heat over medium-high heat. Add shrimp and garlic; stir-fry 3 minutes or until shrimp are pink and opaque. Add green onions; stir-fry 30 seconds. Stir in salsa; heat through. Remove from heat; stir in avocado.

3. Spread beans evenly over warm tostada shells; top with shrimp mixture, lettuce and tomato. *Makes 4 servings*

Bananas

Bananas come in their own handy, easy-open package, making them a perfect take-along snack. Their tropical sweetness adds a bit of sunshine any time of day.

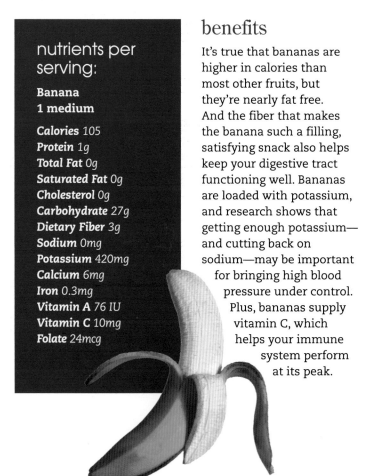

nutrients per serving:

**Banana
1 medium**

Calories 105
Protein 1g
Total Fat 0g
Saturated Fat 0g
Cholesterol 0g
Carbohydrate 27g
Dietary Fiber 3g
Sodium 0mg
Potassium 420mg
Calcium 6mg
Iron 0.3mg
Vitamin A 76 IU
Vitamin C 10mg
Folate 24mcg

benefits

It's true that bananas are higher in calories than most other fruits, but they're nearly fat free. And the fiber that makes the banana such a filling, satisfying snack also helps keep your digestive tract functioning well. Bananas are loaded with potassium, and research shows that getting enough potassium—and cutting back on sodium—may be important for bringing high blood pressure under control. Plus, bananas supply vitamin C, which helps your immune system perform at its peak.

selection and storage

There are different types of bananas, but the yellow Cavendish are the most familiar. Most bananas ripen after picking, and as they do, their starch turns to sugar. So the riper they are, the sweeter they are. Look for plump, firm bananas with no bruises or split skins. Allow bananas to ripen at room temperature. Once they're ripe, refrigerate them to stop the process. The peel will turn brown, but the flesh inside will stay fresh and sweet for a few days.

preparation and serving tips

Bananas are great on their own, but when mashed, they make a great low-fat, nutrient-packed spread for toasted bread or bagels. Sprinkle lemon juice on slices to keep them from darkening. To salvage bananas that are too ripe, peel and freeze them so they're ready when you want a smoothie. They can also be thawed for use in banana bread.

banana split breakfast bowl

2½ tablespoons sliced almonds
2½ tablespoons chopped walnuts
3 cups vanilla fat-free yogurt
1⅓ cups sliced strawberries (about 12 medium)
2 bananas, sliced
½ cup drained pineapple tidbits

1. Spread almonds and walnuts in single layer in small heavy skillet. Cook and stir over medium heat 2 minutes or until nuts are lightly browned. Immediately remove from skillet; let cool before using.

2. Spoon yogurt into individual bowls. Top with strawberries, bananas and pineapple. Sprinkle with almonds and walnuts. *Makes 4 servings*

Note: Breakfast is a great time to eat one of the two recommended fruit servings for the day. This recipe can be made with frozen strawberries or other fruits. Frozen fruits are harvested at their peak and can be stored in the freezer for 8 to 12 months. While fresh is usually better, frozen fruits are nutritious, economical, ready to use and available year-round.

nutrients per serving:

Calories 268
Calories from Fat 17%
Protein 10g
Carbohydrate 50g
Fiber 5g
Total Fat 5g
Saturated Fat <1g
Cholesterol 0mg
Sodium 112mg

Barley

Barley may be best known as a soup ingredient, but this versatile, fiber-rich grain can also be used in casseroles and stews. Its nutty flavor and slightly chewy texture also make barley a satisfying change from rice.

benefits

Barley contains beta-glucan, the same cholesterol-lowering soluble fiber found in oat bran and dried beans. Barley is rich in insoluble fiber as well, absorbing water so it adds bulk and speeds intestinal contents through your body, which may reduce your risk for colorectal cancers. Insoluble fiber may also help keep digestive disorders like constipation at bay.

selection and storage

Hulled (whole grain) barley has only its outer husk removed, so it's the most nutritious variety. Scotch barley is husked and coarsely ground but less refined and more nutritious than the more common pearl (polished) barley. Since its bran has been removed, pearl barley is lower in fiber, vitamins and minerals but is still quite nutritious. It cooks more quickly than hulled or Scotch. Quick barley is pearl barley that's presteamed to cook even faster. Store barley in an airtight container in a cool, dark place.

preparation and serving tips

To cook, add 1 cup pearl barley to 2 cups boiling water or 1 cup hulled barley to 3 cups boiling water. Simmer, covered, until all water is absorbed, 10 to 15 minutes for quick barley, 45 to 55 minutes for pearl or 60 to 90 minutes for hulled. You can soak hulled barley overnight to reduce cooking time. As barley cooks, it absorbs water and swells, so it's an excellent thickener for soups and stews.

nutrients per serving:

Barley, pearl
½ cup cooked

Calories 97
Protein 2g
Total Fat 0g
Saturated Fat 0g
Cholesterol 0g
Carbohydrate 22g
Dietary Fiber 3g
Sodium 0mg
Potassium 73mg
Calcium 9mg
Iron 1mg
Vitamin A 5 IU
Vitamin C 0mg
Folate 13mcg

barley and swiss chard skillet casserole

- **1 cup water**
- **1 cup chopped red bell pepper**
- **1 cup chopped green bell pepper**
- **¾ cup quick-cooking barley**
- **⅛ teaspoon garlic powder**
- **⅛ teaspoon red pepper flakes**
- **2 cups packed coarsely chopped Swiss chard***
- **1 cup canned reduced-sodium navy beans, rinsed and drained**
- **1 cup quartered cherry tomatoes**
- **¼ cup chopped fresh basil leaves**
- **1 tablespoon olive oil**
- **2 tablespoons Italian-seasoned dry bread crumbs**

Fresh spinach or beet greens can be substituted for Swiss chard.

1. Preheat broiler.

2. Bring water to a boil in large ovenproof skillet; add bell peppers, barley, garlic powder and red pepper flakes. Reduce heat; cover and simmer 10 minutes or until liquid is absorbed. Remove from heat.

3. Stir in chard, beans, tomatoes, basil and olive oil. Sprinkle with bread crumbs. Broil 2 minutes or until golden. *Makes 4 servings*

Basil

The spicy fragrance and fresh licorice flavor of basil can transport you to a summer day on the Mediterranean. A relative of mint, basil is the perfect accent in tomato and pasta dishes.

benefits

When you're watching your sodium intake, you'll want basil in the house. Like other herbs, basil is a flavorful and healthy substitute for salt. Fresh basil contains flavonoids and beta-carotene, powerful antioxidants that protect the body's cells from damage that can lead to disease. Basil also contributes magnesium, which promotes cardiovascular health by prompting muscles and blood vessels to relax, improving blood flow throughout the body.

selection and storage

There are more than 60 varieties of basil, all of which differ in appearance and taste. While the taste of sweet basil is bright and pungent, other varieties also offer unique tastes: Lemon basil, anise basil and cinnamon basil all have subtle flavors that reflect their name. Fresh basil is available year-round in many markets. Choose evenly colored leaves with no signs of wilting. Store fresh basil in the refrigerator, wrapped loosely in damp paper towels in a plastic bag or with stems in a glass of water. Use fresh basil within a week. Store dried basil in a cool, dark place for up to six months.

preparation and serving tips

Basil is most well known in pesto, a mixture of basil, olive oil, garlic, pine nuts and Parmesan cheese. It can be used to flavor many types of foods. Be aware that the flavor and aroma of dried basil is different. To substitute fresh for dried, use 1 tablespoon fresh for each teaspoon dried.

nutrients per serving:

Basil, fresh
¼ cup

Calories 1
Protein 0g
Total Fat 0g
Saturated Fat 0g
Cholesterol 0g
Carbohydrate <1g
Dietary Fiber <1g
Sodium 0mg
Potassium 20mg
Calcium 11mg
Iron 0.2mg
Vitamin A 316 IU
Vitamin C 1mg
Folate 4mcg
Magnesium 4mg

mediterranean soup with mozzarella

Nonstick cooking spray

2 medium green bell peppers, chopped

1 cup chopped onion

2 cups (about 8 ounces) chopped eggplant

1 cup (about 4 ounces) sliced mushrooms

6 tablespoons finely chopped fresh basil, divided

2 cloves garlic, minced

3 cups water

1 can (about 14 ounces) diced tomatoes with Italian herbs

½ cup red wine or water

1 can (about 15 ounces) reduced-sodium white beans, rinsed and drained

2 teaspoons sugar

¼ teaspoon salt

1½ cups (6 ounces) shredded reduced-fat mozzarella cheese

1. Spray Dutch oven with cooking spray; heat over medium-high heat. Add bell peppers and onion; cook 4 minutes or until onion is translucent, stirring frequently.

2. Add eggplant, mushrooms, 3 tablespoons basil and garlic; cook and stir 4 minutes. Stir in water, tomatoes and wine. Reduce heat; cover and simmer 30 minutes, stirring occasionally.

3. Remove from heat. Stir in beans, sugar and salt. Cover and let stand 5 minutes. Toss remaining 3 tablespoons basil with cheese in small bowl; top each serving with ¼ cup cheese mixture.

Makes 6 servings

nutrients per serving:

Calories 130
Calories from Fat 22%
Protein 16g
Carbohydrate 9g
Fiber 2g
Total Fat 3g
Saturated Fat 1g
Cholesterol 3mg
Sodium 411mg

Beans

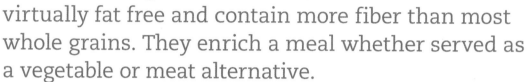

It's hard to beat beans as a healthy, versatile source of essential nutrients. These protein-rich legumes are virtually fat free and contain more fiber than most whole grains. They enrich a meal whether served as a vegetable or meat alternative.

benefits

Many experts recommend we eat 1½ cups of beans a week. One important reason: According to research, diets that include beans are associated with lower risks of heart disease and some cancers. Beans also provide significant amounts of folate, manganese, magnesium, copper, iron and potassium—nutrients many of us get too little of. And their protein and iron make beans all but essential for people who don't eat meat.

selection and storage

Beans come in a variety of shapes, colors and sizes and are often interchangeable in recipes. Dried beans are inexpensive, but they require more time to prepare. For convenience, you'll find many types of cooked beans available in cans. Dried beans last for a year or more in an airtight container. Store cooked beans in the refrigerator up to one week or in the freezer up to six months.

preparation and serving tips

Beans may be bland tasting, but they take on the seasoning of any dish. Many cultures have perfected the art of combining beans with grains or seeds to provide a nutritionally complete protein. Try Mexican corn tortillas with beans or classic Spanish rice and beans. Using beans in a recipe can be as easy as opening a can, draining and rinsing (to reduce sodium by at least 40 percent). If you use dried beans, be sure to allow time and follow the instructions for sorting, rinsing, soaking and cooking.

nutrients per serving:

Beans, kidney ½ cup cooked

Calories 112
Protein 8g
Total Fat 0g
Saturated Fat 0g
Cholesterol 0g
Carbohydrate 20g
Dietary Fiber 6g
Sodium 0mg
Potassium 360mg
Iron 2mg
Folate 115mcg
Magnesium 37mg
Manganese 0.4mg
Copper 0.2mg

black bean burgers

- 2 cans (about 15 ounces each) black beans, rinsed and drained, divided
- ¾ cup plain dry bread crumbs
- ⅔ cup coarsely chopped green onions
- 2 egg whites
- ¼ cup chopped fresh basil
- 2 teaspoons onion powder
- 2 teaspoons dried oregano
- 1 teaspoon baking powder
- 1 teaspoon ground cumin
- 1 teaspoon black pepper
- ½ teaspoon salt
- ¾ cup corn
- ¾ cup chopped roasted red pepper
- 6 whole wheat hamburger buns
  Salsa (optional)
  Avocado slices (optional)

1. Place half of beans in food processor. Add bread crumbs, green onions, egg whites, basil, onion powder, oregano, baking powder, cumin, black pepper and salt. Pulse 30 to 40 seconds or until mixture begins to hold together. Fold in remaining beans, corn and roasted red pepper. Let stand at room temperature 20 minutes for flavors to develop.

2. Preheat oven to 350°F. Line baking sheet with parchment paper.

3. Shape mixture into 6 patties (about ½ cup each). Place patties on prepared baking sheet. Bake 18 to 20 minutes or until patties are firm. Serve on buns; top with salsa and avocado, if desired.

Makes 6 servings

nutrients per serving:

Calories 149
Calories from Fat 9%
Protein 7g
Carbohydrate 31g
Fiber 6g
Total Fat 2g
Saturated Fat <1g
Cholesterol 0mg
Sodium 696mg

Beef Tenderloin

Surprise! Beef tenderloin contains only 8 grams of fat per 3 ounces—that's less than a skinless chicken thigh. You probably don't need convincing that this luxurious cut of beef makes for a rich and satisfying meal.

nutrients per serving:

Beef Tenderloin, trimmed
3 ounces roasted

Calories 174
Protein 23g
Total Fat 8g
Saturated Fat 3g
Cholesterol 72g
Carbohydrate 0g
Dietary Fiber 0g
Sodium 50mg
Potassium 280mg
Iron 1.4mg
Zinc 4.2mg
Phosphorus 184mg
Vitamin B6 0.5mg
Vitamin B12 1.2mcg

benefits

Lean beef is highly nutritious, providing quality protein and essential vitamins and minerals. Beef's easily absorbed iron is especially valuable, since a shortage of this mineral is the most common nutritional deficiency and leading cause of anemia in the United States. Half the fat in beef is monounsaturated, the same heart-healthy fat in olive oil. And a third of beef's saturated fat is a unique type shown to have a neutral effect on blood cholesterol. Short- and long-term studies indicate lean beef can fit in diets for lowering blood cholesterol.

selection and storage

Choose beef with a bright cherry-red or purplish color without any gray or brown blotches. Purchase tightly sealed packages before or on the "sell by" date on the package. Refrigerate or freeze beef as soon as possible after purchase. Use refrigerated beef within four days after purchase. To keep beef tenderloin lean, trim all fat from the exterior. To find other lean beef cuts, look for "loin" or "round" in the name.

preparation and serving tips

Tender beef cuts, like tenderloin, are best prepared with a dry-heat cooking method such as roasting, grilling, broiling or stir-frying. These methods require little or no added fat. When using a marinade, tender cuts need only 15 minutes to 2 hours to add flavor. A seasoning rub is another great way to add flavor to the surface of beef. Cook to an internal temperature of at least 145°F (medium rare) for food safety.

beef tenderloin with spice rub

1 tablespoon onion powder
2 teaspoons dried thyme
1 teaspoon ground cumin
¾ teaspoon ground allspice
1 teaspoon black pepper or lemon pepper
½ teaspoon salt
⅛ teaspoon ground red pepper
  Nonstick cooking spray
2 pounds beef tenderloin
¼ cup water

1. Combine onion powder, thyme, cumin, allspice, black pepper, salt and red pepper in small bowl. Sprinkle evenly over all sides of beef. Press down firmly to allow seasonings to adhere. Wrap tightly in plastic wrap and refrigerate 24 hours.

2. Preheat oven to 400°F. Spray nonstick baking pan with cooking spray.

3. Spray large skillet with cooking spray; heat over medium-high heat. Add beef; cook 5 minutes, turning to brown all sides. Transfer beef to prepared baking pan. Add water to skillet; cook and stir 15 seconds, scraping up brown bits. Drizzle over beef.

4. Bake 25 minutes or until meat thermometer registers 145°F or desired degree of doneness.

5. Tent with foil and let stand 5 minutes. Place beef on cutting board; slice and serve with pan drippings.   *Makes 8 servings*

Bell Peppers

Bell peppers, also known as sweet peppers, come in a rainbow of colors—green, yellow, orange, red, purple and brown. Flavors range from herbal-tasting green peppers to red peppers that are amazingly sweet.

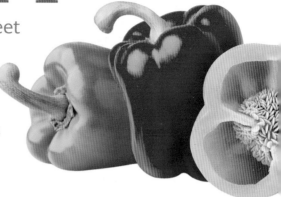

benefits

Bell peppers, especially red ones, actually provide more vitamin C than citrus fruits do. They're brimming with vitamin A, too. Both vitamins act as antioxidants, supporting our immune function and helping protect us from cell damage, inflammation, cancer and diseases related to aging. Bell peppers also supply the antioxidant lutein, which has been linked to reduced risk of the sight-stealing disease macular degeneration. The deep colors sported by bell peppers signal their rich reserves of plant pigments that help fight cancer. Peppers even provide a decent amount of fiber.

selection and storage

Green peppers are simply red peppers that haven't completely ripened. Once ripe, they are more perishable and carry a premium price. Look for a glossy sheen and no shriveling, cracks or soft spots. Bell peppers should feel heavy for their size, indicating fully developed walls. Store in a plastic bag in your refrigerator's crisper drawer. Green peppers stay firm for a week; others go soft in three or four days.

preparation and serving tips

Bell peppers are delicious raw—in a salad, with a low-fat dip or as a snack. Core bell peppers and steam them to make beautiful containers for stuffings of all kinds. Bell peppers are also great on the grill. Grill large pieces until the outer skin is blackened and then rub it off when they cool.

nutrients per serving:

**Bell Peppers, red
½ cup raw slices**

Calories 14
Protein 1g
Total Fat 0g
Saturated Fat 0g
Cholesterol 0g
Carbohydrate 3g
Dietary Fiber 1g
Sodium 0mg
Potassium 97mg
Calcium 3mg
Iron 0.2mg
Vitamin A 1,440 IU
Vitamin C 59mg
Folate 21mcg

fajita salad

- ¼ cup fresh lime juice
- 2 tablespoons chopped fresh cilantro
- 1 clove garlic, minced
- 1 teaspoon chili powder
- 6 ounces boneless beef top sirloin steak, cut into strips
- 1 teaspoon olive oil
- 2 medium red bell peppers, cut into strips
- 1 medium onion, sliced
- 1 cup canned chickpeas, rinsed and drained
- 4 cups mixed salad greens
- 1 medium tomato, cut into wedges
- 1 cup salsa

nutrients per serving:

Calories 181
Calories from Fat 18%
Protein 16g
Carbohydrate 25g
Fiber 6g
Total Fat 4g
Saturated Fat 1g
Cholesterol 22mg
Sodium 698mg

1. Combine lime juice, cilantro, garlic and chili powder in large resealable food storage bag. Add beef; seal bag. Let stand 10 minutes, turning once.

2. Heat oil in large nonstick skillet over medium-high heat. Add bell peppers and onion; cook and stir 6 minutes or until vegetables are crisp-tender. Remove from skillet.

3. Add beef and marinade to skillet; cook and stir 3 minutes or until beef is cooked through. Remove from heat. Add bell pepper mixture and chickpeas to skillet; toss to coat with pan juices. Cool slightly.

4. Divide salad greens evenly among serving plates. Top with beef mixture and tomato wedges. Serve with salsa. *Makes 4 servings*

Blackberries

Blackberries taste so good it's hard to believe they're so good for you. Sweet, ripe blackberries need no accompaniment other than a napkin to wipe the luscious juices from your chin.

nutrients per serving:

Blackberries
½ cup

Calories 31
Protein 1g
Total Fat 0g
Saturated Fat 0g
Cholesterol 0g
Carbohydrate 7g
Dietary Fiber 4g
Sodium 0mg
Potassium 120mg
Calcium 21mg
Iron 0.5mg
Vitamin A 154 IU
Vitamin C 15mg
Folate 18mcg

benefits

Fresh blackberries are an excellent source of vitamin C, which is essential for strong immunity and healthy blood vessels, bones and teeth. And thanks to all those little seeds, blackberries have more fiber than a serving of some whole grain cereals. These delightful berries are low in calories and packed with soluble fiber that helps slow absorption of sugar and cholesterol from food. The dark pigment that gives blackberries their midnight hue comes from high levels of anthocyanins and ellagic acid—phytonutrients with a grocery list of health benefits, such as helping to ward off heart disease and cancer and combating some of the negative effects of aging.

selection and storage

Look for berries that are glossy, plump and firm. The darker the berries, the riper and sweeter they are. Refrigerate blackberries, but don't wash them until you're ready to eat them. Enjoy them as soon as possible since they only last a day or two. For a midwinter pick-up, freeze washed and dried berries in a single layer on a baking sheet. Once frozen, store in an airtight container and thaw as needed.

preparation and serving tips

Pick through to remove stems and berries that are too soft and wash them gently under running water. Overhandling can crush cell walls, releasing juice and nutrients. Serve blackberries over cereal, yogurt or sorbet. Bake them into a fruit crisp or cobbler for a delicious dessert.

blackberry custard pie

Pie Crust (recipe follows)
½ cup sugar
3 tablespoons cornstarch
1¼ cups low-fat (1%) milk
2 teaspoons grated lemon peel
1 tablespoon lemon juice
2 eggs, lightly beaten
1 pint blackberries

nutrients per serving:

Calories 245
Calories from Fat 32%
Protein 5g
Carbohydrate 37g
Fiber 3g

Total Fat 9g
Saturated Fat 1g
Cholesterol 55mg
Sodium 54mg

1. Preheat oven to 425°F. Prepare Pie Crust. Pierce crust with fork at ¼-inch intervals, about 40 times. Cut square of foil about 4 inches larger than pie plate. Line crust with foil; fill with dried beans, uncooked rice or pie weights. Bake 10 minutes or until set.

2. Remove crust from oven; gently remove foil and beans. Return crust to oven; bake 5 minutes or until light brown. Cool completely on wire rack.

3. Combine sugar and cornstarch in small saucepan. Stir in milk, lemon peel and lemon juice; cook and stir over medium heat until mixture boils and thickens. Boil 1 minute, stirring constantly. Stir about ½ cup hot milk mixture into eggs; stir egg mixture back into saucepan. Cook over low heat until thickened, stirring constantly. Spoon hot custard into pie crust. Cool to room temperature; refrigerate about 3 hours or until set. Arrange blackberries on custard.

Makes 8 servings

pie crust

1¼ cups all-purpose flour
¼ teaspoon baking powder
Dash salt
¼ cup canola or vegetable oil
3 tablespoons fat-free (skim) milk, divided

1. Combine flour, baking powder and salt in medium bowl. Add oil and 2 tablespoons milk; mix well. Add enough remaining milk to hold mixture together. Shape dough into a ball.

2. Flatten dough to 1-inch thickness on 12-inch square of waxed paper; cover with second square of waxed paper. Roll out to form 12-inch round crust. Mend tears by pressing together with fingers. Remove top layer of waxed paper. Place dough, paper side up, in 9-inch pie pan. Peel off remaining paper. Press into pan and flute edge.

Blueberries

Blueberries belong at breakfast, lunch or dinner. These powerfully nutritious little berries add color and flavor to everything from pancakes to salads to blueberry pie.

benefits

Blueberries are antioxidant superstars, ranking second among top antioxidant-rich foods. Emerging research shows the antioxidants in blueberries may protect brain cells and help reverse age-related memory loss. In addition, blueberries contain anthocyanins, the phytonutrients that give them their distinctive blue-purple color and may help prevent heart disease and cancer. Blueberries also provide both iron and vitamin C, an especially beneficial combination because vitamin C enables the body to better absorb the iron in plant foods. And like their family members cranberries, blueberries can help treat and prevent urinary tract infections.

selection and storage

Blueberries are at their best from May through October when they are in season. Choose blueberries that are firm, uniform in size and indigo blue with a silvery frost. Sort and discard shriveled or moldy berries. Do not wash until ready to use, and store in a moisture-proof container in the refrigerator for up to five days. Freeze washed and dried blueberries in a single layer on a baking sheet; place in a sealed bag or container once frozen.

preparation and serving tips

Enjoy blueberries when they are in season—on cereal or yogurt, in salads, with a splash of cream or simply out of hand. Frozen blueberries make a refreshing snack on a hot day and a great addition to smoothies. Blueberries are easy to bake into muffins, pancakes, quick breads, pies, cobblers and fruit crisps. Use blueberries to make jam for a nutritious low-fat spread for toast or crackers. Once frozen, use blueberries in baking since they become mushy when thawed.

nutrients per serving:

Blueberries
½ cup

Calories 42
Protein 1g
Total Fat 0g
Saturated Fat 0g

Cholesterol 0g
Carbohydrate 11g
Dietary Fiber 2g
Sodium 0mg
Potassium 60mg
Calcium 4mg

Iron 0.2mg
Vitamin A 40 IU
Vitamin C 7mg
Folate 4mcg

blueberry soy shake

½ cup plus 2 tablespoons soymilk
¼ cup crushed ice
2 tablespoons fresh or frozen
   blueberries (about 20 berries)
¼ teaspoon unsweetened cocoa
   powder

1. Combine soymilk, ice, blueberries and cocoa in blender. Blend 30 seconds or until smooth.

2. Pour into chilled glass. Serve immediately.   *Makes 1 serving*

nutrients per serving:

Calories 99
Calories from Fat 26%
Protein 5g
Carbohydrate 14g
Fiber 2g
Total Fat 3g
Saturated Fat <1g
Cholesterol 0mg
Sodium 79mg

Bok Choy

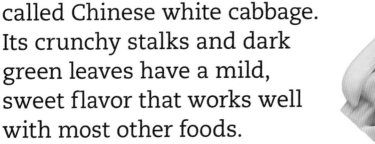

Bok choy, or pak choi, is sometimes called Chinese white cabbage. Its crunchy stalks and dark green leaves have a mild, sweet flavor that works well with most other foods.

nutrients per serving:

Bok Choy
½ cup cooked

Calories 10
Protein 1g
Total Fat 0g
Saturated Fat 0g
Cholesterol 0g
Carbohydrate 2g
Dietary Fiber 1g
Sodium 29mg
Potassium 315mg
Calcium 79mg
Iron 0.9mg
Vitamin A 3,612 IU
Vitamin C 22mg
Folate 35mcg

benefits

Bok choy is one valuable cabbage when it comes to controlling blood pressure. That's because it provides ample potassium and a well-absorbed, nondairy source of calcium, two minerals essential for healthy blood pressure. What's more, unlike many plant sources of calcium, bok choy is low in oxalates, substances that reduce calcium absorption in the body. As its dark green color suggests, bok choy is also rich in beta-carotene, an antioxidant warrior in the battles against heart disease and cancer.

selection and storage

Bok choy is available year-round in most supermarkets. Choose bok choy with firm stalks topped with crisp, dark green leaves. Avoid bunches with browning stalks or wilted leaves. It should be refrigerated in a plastic bag and used within three to four days.

preparation and serving tips

Bok choy is a versatile cabbage that can be enjoyed raw or cooked. Remove the bottom of the bok choy plant with a sharp knife so the stalks separate. Rinse the leaves with cool water and pat dry. The crisp stalks and tender leaves make a nice addition to a salad. For a stir-fry, chop the stems and leaves separately into small pieces. Add the stems first since they require longer cooking time. For a side dish, sauté chopped bok choy with soy sauce, a dash of sesame oil and your seasoning of choice, such as garlic, lemon juice, dried chili peppers or ginger.

thai-style beef with pasta on lettuce

- 3 tablespoons orange juice
- 2 tablespoons creamy peanut butter
- 2 tablespoons reduced-sodium soy sauce
- 1 tablespoon unseasoned rice vinegar
- 2 teaspoons grated fresh ginger
- 6 ounces uncooked whole wheat spaghetti, broken in half
- ½ pound 95% lean ground beef
- 2 teaspoons minced garlic
- 2 cups (about 4 ounces) thinly sliced bok choy
- ½ cup (about 2 ounces) coarsely chopped carrot
- 4 green onions, cut into 1-inch pieces
- ¼ teaspoon red pepper flakes
  Leaf lettuce
- 2 tablespoons (½ ounce) dry roasted peanuts

1. Process orange juice, peanut butter, soy sauce, vinegar and ginger in food processor or blender until nearly smooth. Set aside.

2. Cook spaghetti according to package directions; drain and keep warm.

3. Meanwhile, brown beef and garlic in large nonstick skillet over medium-high heat 6 to 8 minutes, stirring to break up meat. Drain fat. Stir in bok choy, carrot, green onions and red pepper flakes. Drizzle with orange juice mixture. Reduce heat to medium; cover and cook 2 minutes.

4. Add hot spaghetti; toss until combined. Place lettuce leaves on serving plates. Spoon beef mixture onto lettuce and sprinkle with peanuts.   *Makes 6 servings*

nutrients per serving:

Calories 219
Calories from Fat 29%
Protein 15g

Carbohydrate 27g
Fiber 1g
Total Fat 7g
Saturated Fat 2g
Cholesterol 23mg
Sodium 285mg

Broccoli

Beautiful, beneficial broccoli provides a hefty dose of disease-fighting nutrients for very few calories. As a side or in a salad, soup or stir-fry, broccoli complements other flavors and textures.

benefits

Broccoli's noteworthy nutrients include vitamin C, vitamin A (mostly as the antioxidant beta-carotene), folate, calcium and fiber. That resumé is especially beneficial for women, since adequate folate intake before and during pregnancy helps prevent neural-tube birth defects. And getting enough calcium can help prevent osteoporosis. Broccoli is rich in various phytonutrients that serve as powerful cancer fighters, helping to inhibit tumor growth and boost the action of protective enzymes.

Research has shown that people who eat broccoli and other cruciferous vegetables regularly have a significantly reduced incidence of cancer.

selection and storage

Look for broccoli that's dark green or even purplish green but not yellow. Florets should be compact and of even color. Leaves should not be wilted and stalks should not be fat and woody. The greener it is, the more beta-carotene it has. Store unwashed broccoli in a plastic bag in your refrigerator's crisper drawer. Use within a few days.

preparation and serving tips

Wash broccoli just before using. Steaming is the best way to retain broccoli's nutrients. Prevent any unpleasant odor by not overcooking. Steam only until crisp-tender, about 5 minutes. Broccoli florets can boost the nutrition, flavor and color of any stir-fry dish. Raw broccoli is great tossed into salads or as a finger food with a low-fat dip. For a healthy side dish, skip the cheese sauce. Instead, add a squeeze of lemon and a dusting of cracked pepper or a drizzle of olive oil.

nutrients per serving:

Broccoli
½ cup cooked

Calories 27
Protein 2g
Total Fat 0g
Saturated Fat 0g
Cholesterol 0g
Carbohydrate 6g
Dietary Fiber 3g
Sodium 32mg
Potassium 229mg
Calcium 31mg
Iron 0.5mg
Vitamin A 1,207 IU
Vitamin C 51mg
Folate 84mcg

crustless salmon & broccoli quiche

¾ cup cholesterol-free egg
    substitute
¼ cup chopped green onions
¼ cup plain fat-free yogurt
2 teaspoons all-purpose flour
1 teaspoon dried basil
⅛ teaspoon salt
⅛ teaspoon black pepper
¾ cup frozen broccoli florets,
    thawed and drained
⅓ cup (3 ounces) drained and
    flaked canned salmon
2 tablespoons grated Parmesan
    cheese
1 plum tomato, thinly sliced
¼ cup fresh bread crumbs

1. Preheat oven to 375°F. Spray
1½-quart casserole or 9-inch deep-
dish pie plate with nonstick cooking
spray.

2. Combine egg substitute, green onions, yogurt,
flour, basil, salt and pepper in medium bowl until
well blended. Stir in broccoli, salmon and cheese.
Spread evenly in prepared casserole. Top with
tomato slices and sprinkle with bread crumbs.

3. Bake 20 to 25 minutes or until knife inserted into
center comes out clean. Let stand 5 minutes before
serving. *Makes 4 servings*

Broccoli Rabe

Despite its name, this distant cousin of broccoli is more closely related to turnips and cabbage. The somewhat bitter flavor is much appreciated in Italy and is growing in popularity here. It's also known as broccoli raab or rapini.

nutrients per serving:

Broccoli Rabe
½ cup cooked

Calories 38
Protein 4g
Total Fat 0.5g
Saturated Fat 0g
Cholesterol 0g
Carbohydrate 4g
Dietary Fiber 3g
Sodium 64mg
Potassium 390mg
Calcium 136mg
Iron 1.5mg
Vitamin A 5,213 IU
Vitamin C 43mg
Folate 82mcg

benefits

Like other cruciferous vegetables, broccoli rabe offers a wealth of health-promoting nutrients for a very small calorie price. Just ½ cup provides more than 10 percent of the recommended daily intakes of fiber, potassium, folate and calcium and more than 50 percent of daily needs for vitamins A and C. As a bonus, it's stuffed with potent cancer-fighting phytonutrients.

selection and storage

Broccoli rabe can be found from fall to spring in markets with specialty produce sections. Look for broccoli rabe that is bright green with firm, crisp leaves, broccoli-like buds and thin stalks, with no yellowing or spotting. It should be wrapped loosely in a plastic bag and refrigerated for no more than five days. After cooking, refrigerate in a sealed container for up to two days.

preparation and serving tips

Rabe is a bitter green and may be an acquired taste. To soften the pungency, blanch it for 30 to 60 seconds in boiling water, then cook as directed. To prepare broccoli rabe, remove an inch of the stems and peel the lower half of any very thick ones to reduce toughness. The simplest way to cook broccoli rabe is to sauté in olive oil with minced garlic and a pinch of red pepper flakes. The hearty flavor holds its own even with heavily spiced entrées.

Brussels Sprouts

These cute miniature cabbages share many of the health benefits of their larger cousins. In season, you can often purchase fresh brussels sprouts as they grow, clustered around a single long stalk.

benefits

Brussels sprouts are a nutritional bargain. In just ½ cup of these hearty little heads, you get a decent amount of protein and fiber but few calories, minimal sodium and no fat. Plus, like cabbage and other cruciferous veggies, brussels sprouts come loaded with a package of potent phytonutrients that may help protect your body against cancer. They are rich in vitamin C, which plays a vital role in helping your body ward off infections, and are also a good source of potassium, iron and vitamin A.

selection and storage

Fresh brussels sprouts shine in fall and winter. Look for a pronounced green color and tight, compact, firm heads. The fewer the yellowed, wilted or loose leaves the better. Smaller sprouts are more tender and flavorful. Pick ones of similar size so they cook evenly. Stored in the refrigerator in a loosely closed plastic bag, they'll last a week or two.

preparation and serving tips

Rinse brussels sprouts under running water, then pull off loose or wilted leaves and trim the stem ends a little. Cut an "X" in the bottoms to help them cook evenly. Steaming is better than boiling to preserve nutrients and minimize odor. Cook just until tender. Another way to prepare brussels sprouts is to cut in half lengthwise, toss with olive oil, salt and pepper and roast in a 400°F oven until crisp and tender. Roasted brussels sprouts are delicious served with just a squeeze of lemon.

nutrients per serving:

Brussels Sprouts ½ cup cooked		
Calories 28	Cholesterol 0g	
Protein 2g	Carbohydrate 6g	
Total Fat 0g	Dietary Fiber 2g	Iron 0.9mg
Saturated Fat 0g	Sodium 15mg	Vitamin A 604 IU
	Potassium 245mg	Vitamin C 48mg
	Calcium 28mg	Folate 47mcg

Buckwheat

Despite its name, buckwheat is not wheat. It's the seed from an herb plant that is ground into flour and most commonly used in pancakes or blini. When hulled and crushed, it's called buckwheat groats. Toasted groats are known as kasha.

nutrients per serving:

Buckwheat, kasha
½ cup cooked

Calories 77
Protein 3g
Total Fat 0.5g
Saturated Fat 0g
Cholesterol 0g
Carbohydrate 17g
Dietary Fiber 2g
Sodium 0mg
Potassium 70mg
Calcium 6mg
Iron 0.7mg
Magnesium 43mg
Folate 12mcg

benefits

Buckwheat contains more protein—and more nutritionally complete protein—than grains do. That makes buckwheat especially beneficial for people who avoid or limit meat and/or other animal products, the only foods that provide complete proteins. Buckwheat is an excellent source of magnesium, which is essential for healthy blood pressure. And buckwheat contains a phytochemical and known cancer fighter called rutin that also helps reduce cholesterol and strengthen blood vessels.

selection and storage

You can buy buckwheat groats whole or cracked into coarse, medium or fine grinds, or roasted as kasha. Very finely cracked, unroasted groats, or buckwheat grits, are sold for hot cereal. Buckwheat is also used to make Japanese soba noodles. Store buckwheat in a well-sealed container. At room temperature, it is susceptible to turning rancid, so store it in the refrigerator or freezer.

preparation and serving tips

Buckwheat has an intense, nutty flavor. You can substitute buckwheat groats or kasha in some recipes calling for rice or other whole grains. Cook groats or kasha like rice, using 2 cups of liquid for each cup of groats. Buckwheat flour is superb for pancakes, but not for bread because it contains no gluten to provide structure. You can add ¼ to ½ cup of buckwheat flour to a recipe for bread as long as the primary grain is wheat.

spicy sesame noodles

6 ounces uncooked soba (buckwheat) noodles

2 teaspoons dark sesame oil

1 tablespoon sesame seeds

½ cup fat-free reduced-sodium chicken broth

1 tablespoon creamy peanut butter

½ cup thinly sliced green onions

½ cup minced red bell pepper

4 teaspoons reduced-sodium soy sauce

1½ teaspoons finely chopped seeded jalapeño pepper*

1 clove garlic, minced

¼ teaspoon red pepper flakes

Jalapeño peppers can sting and irritate the skin, so wear rubber gloves when handling peppers and do not touch your eyes.

1. Cook noodles according to package directions. (Do not overcook.) Rinse noodles thoroughly with cold water; drain. Place noodles in large bowl; toss with oil.

2. Place sesame seeds in small skillet. Cook over medium heat about 3 minutes or until seeds begin to pop and turn golden brown, stirring frequently. Remove from heat; set aside.

3. Whisk broth and peanut butter in small bowl until blended. (Mixture may look curdled.) Stir in green onions, bell pepper, soy sauce, jalapeño pepper, garlic and red pepper flakes.

4. Pour mixture over noodles; toss to coat. Cover and let stand at room temperature 30 minutes or refrigerate up to 24 hours. Sprinkle with toasted sesame seeds before serving.

Makes 6 servings

nutrients per serving:

Calories 145
Calories from Fat 23%
Protein 6g
Carbohydrate 24g
Fiber 1g
Total Fat 4g
Saturated Fat 1g
Cholesterol 0mg
Sodium 358mg

Bulgur

This Middle Eastern staple consists of wheat kernels that have been steamed, dried and crushed. Bulgur wheat has a mild flavor, cooks quickly and takes well to many different seasonings. It deserves a place in your healthful meal plan.

benefits

Being minimally processed, bulgur remains high in protein, fiber and minerals, just like whole wheat. It's tastier and more nutritious than white rice and actually has more fiber and fewer calories than brown rice. It also doesn't cause large spikes in blood sugar. It's a hearty, fat-free foundation for healthy meals. Plus, bulgur's insoluble fiber absorbs water in the digestive tract, promoting faster elimination of waste, which helps limit contact with potentially cancer-causing agents.

selection and storage

Bulgur is available in three grinds—coarse, medium and fine. Coarse bulgur is used to make pilaf or stuffing. Medium-grind bulgur is used in cereals. The finest grind of bulgur is suited to the popular cold Middle Eastern salad called tabbouleh. Store bulgur in a screw-top glass jar in the refrigerator; it will keep for months.

preparation and serving tips

Because bulgur is already partially cooked, little time is needed for preparation. The method depends on the grind of bulgur and what you'll be using it for, but the general rule is to use a two to one ratio of liquid to bulgur. Fine bulgur can usually be cooked by adding boiling water and letting it sit, covered, for 10 to 15 minutes. Fluff with a fork and you're ready to enjoy bulgur's nutty flavor in place of rice, potatoes or other less nutrient-rich choices.

nutrients per serving:

Bulgur
½ cup cooked

Calories 76
Protein 3g
Total Fat 0g
Saturated Fat 0g
Cholesterol 0mg
Carbohydrate 17g
Dietary Fiber 4g
Sodium 5mg
Potassium 60mg
Calcium 9mg
Iron 0.9mg
Folate 16mcg

chicken with curried bulgur

1¼ cups water, divided
½ teaspoon salt, divided
½ cup uncooked bulgur wheat
4 boneless skinless chicken breasts
    (about ¼ pound each)
½ teaspoon ground cumin, divided
¼ teaspoon black pepper
    Nonstick cooking spray
½ cup raisins
¼ cup slivered almonds, toasted*
¼ cup chopped green onions, divided
½ teaspoon curry powder
½ teaspoon grated fresh ginger

*To toast almonds, spread in shallow baking pan. Bake in preheated 350°F oven 5 to 7 minutes or until fragrant, stirring occasionally.

1. Bring 1 cup water and ¼ teaspoon salt to a boil in small saucepan over high heat; stir in bulgur. Cover; remove from heat and let stand 10 minutes or until liquid is absorbed and bulgur is tender.

2. Meanwhile, sprinkle chicken with remaining ¼ teaspoon salt, ¼ teaspoon cumin and black pepper. Spray large skillet with cooking spray; heat over medium-high heat. Cook chicken 4 to 5 minutes on each side or until no longer pink in center. Remove from skillet; keep warm.

3. Combine remaining ¼ cup water, raisins, almonds, 2 tablespoons green onion, curry powder, ginger and remaining ¼ teaspoon cumin in skillet. Bring to a boil. Reduce heat; fluff bulgur and add to skillet, tossing until combined.

4. Serve chicken on bulgur mixture; sprinkle with remaining 2 tablespoons green onion.

Makes 4 servings

nutrients per serving:

Calories 301	**Total Fat** 7g
Calories from Fat 19%	**Saturated Fat** 1g
Protein 30g	**Cholesterol** 66mg
Carbohydrate 32g	**Sodium** 430mg
Fiber 5g	

Butternut Squash

Sweet and buttery tasting, this winter squash is an excellent choice for flavor and nutrition. Its tough shell allows for longer storage without compromising quality.

nutrients per serving:

Butternut Squash
½ cup cooked

Calories 41
Protein 1g
Total Fat 0g
Saturated Fat 0g
Cholesterol 0mg
Carbohydrate 11g
Dietary Fiber 3.5g
Sodium 0mg
Potassium 290mg
Calcium 42mg
Iron 0.6mg
Vitamin A 11,434 IU
Vitamin C 16mg
Folate 19mcg

benefits

Butternut squash is a gold mine of beta-carotene, its orange-yellow color broadcasting its rich stores of this multitalented form of vitamin A. Beta-carotene is a potent antioxidant that protects the body's cells from harm caused by exposure to tobacco, sunlight, radiation and other potentially cancer-causing substances. It's also a good source of vitamin C, another natural antioxidant that helps shield the body from insults that can trigger cancerous changes and damage blood vessels. Vitamin C is also essential for a healthy immune system.

selection and storage

Butternut squash is available year-round, but its peak season is fall through winter. Choose a squash that is firm and free of bruises, punctures or cuts. Whole squash does not need refrigeration and can be stored in a cool, dark place for several weeks. You can also purchase butternut squash frozen or precut in the refrigerated produce department.

preparation and serving tips

The simplest way to prepare butternut squash is to cut it in half and bake or microwave it. Because the skin is so tough, use caution and a sharp knife to cut the squash. To help soften it for easier cutting, microwave the squash for 3 to 5 minutes. Cut it in half lengthwise, then scoop out the seeds and proceed with cooking or peeling. Add butternut squash to soups or stews, or serve it as a side with a little brown sugar or garlic and Parmesan cheese.

winter squash risotto

2 tablespoons olive oil
2 cups butternut squash (1 small squash), peeled and cut into 1-inch pieces
1 large shallot or small onion, finely chopped
½ teaspoon paprika
¼ teaspoon salt
¼ teaspoon dried thyme
¼ teaspoon black pepper
1 cup uncooked arborio rice
¼ cup dry white wine (optional)
4 to 5 cups hot reduced-sodium vegetable broth
½ cup grated Parmesan or Romano cheese

1. Heat oil in large skillet over medium heat. Add squash; cook and stir 3 minutes. Add shallot; cook and stir 3 to 4 minutes or until squash is almost tender. Stir in paprika, salt, thyme and pepper. Add rice; stir to coat.

2. Add wine, if desired; cook and stir until wine evaporates. Add ½ cup broth; cook, stirring occasionally. When rice is almost dry, stir in another ½ cup broth. Continue to stir rice occasionally, adding ½ cup broth each time previous addition is absorbed. Rice is done when consistency is creamy and grains are tender with slight resistance. (Total cooking time will be 20 to 30 minutes.)

3. Sprinkle with Parmesan cheese and additional salt, if desired. Serve immediately.

Makes 4 to 6 servings

nutrients per serving:

Calories 228
Calories from Fat 27%
Protein 8g
Carbohydrate 35g
Fiber 4g
Total Fat 7g
Saturated Fat 2g
Cholesterol 6mg
Sodium 573mg

Cantaloupe

It's hard to say no to melon with its soft, sweet, juicy flesh and superb taste. And there's no need to, because cantaloupe's nutrient-packed flesh is the perfect substitute for sugary, processed snacks and desserts.

nutrients per serving:

Cantaloupe
½ cup

Calories 27
Protein 1g
Total Fat 0g
Saturated Fat 0g
Cholesterol 0mg
Carbohydrate 7g
Dietary Fiber 1g
Sodium 10mg
Potassium 210mg
Calcium 7mg
Iron 0.2mg
Vitamin A 2,706 IU
Vitamin C 29mg
Folate 17mcg

benefits

Cantaloupe is a good source of potassium, an essential nutrient that may help lower high blood pressure, regulate heartbeat and prevent strokes and heart disease.

But this succulent melon's potential to protect doesn't stop there. Cantaloupe is also rich in beta-carotene, vitamin C and phytonutrients, a powerful trio that helps prevent cardiovascular disease, cancer and infection. Because it's mostly water, cantaloupe is low in calories, yet its fiber content and sweet taste make it satisfying to the taste buds and tummy.

selection and storage

Look for evenly shaped cantaloupe without bruises, cracks or soft spots. Select fruit heavy for its size, which tends to be juicier. Ripe cantaloupe has a mildly sweet fragrance. If the cantaloupe smells sickeningly sweet, or if there is mold where the stem used to be, it is probably overripe and quite possibly rotten. Cantaloupe continues to ripen off the vine, so if you buy it ripe, eat it as soon as possible.

preparation and serving tips

Enjoy refreshing cantaloupe slightly chilled or at room temperature for the most flavor. Chilled melon soup is a refreshing change of pace in hot weather. And the natural cavity left in a cantaloupe after removing the seeds is a perfect place for fillers like nonfat yogurt or fruit salad. Squeeze a little lemon or lime juice onto cut melon for extra flavor.

cantaloupe sorbet

6 cups cubed fresh cantaloupe
⅓ cup light corn syrup
3 tablespoons lime juice

1. Process cantaloupe in food processor until puréed. (You should have about 3 cups.) Add corn syrup and lime juice; process until combined.

2. Freeze cantaloupe mixture in ice cream maker according to manufacturer's directions.

Makes 8 servings

Carrots

Sweet, crunchy carrots are one of America's everyday vegetables, but they are anything but ordinary when it comes to nutrition. Maybe we should amend that well-known saying to: A carrot a day keeps the doctor away.

benefits

Carrots have a well-deserved reputation for being good for the eyes. Their enormous cache of vitamin A (as beta-carotene) helps protect eyesight, including night vision, and helps prevent macular degeneration and cataracts, two leading causes of blindness in people 55 and older. That same vitamin A also helps to keep the skin healthy and supple and the body shielded from infections of all kinds. It's a potent cancer fighter, too. And carrots' soluble fiber helps to lower blood cholesterol levels.

selection and storage

Look for firm, bright orange carrots with smooth skin. Avoid carrots that are limp or black near the top; they're not fresh. Choose medium-sized ones that taper at the end; thicker ones may be tough. In general, early carrots are more tender but less sweet than larger, mature carrots. Baby-cut carrots are sweet and convenient. Carrots keep for a few weeks in the crisper drawer.

preparation and serving tips

Thoroughly wash and scrub whole carrots to remove soil contaminants. To remove pesticide residues, peel the outer layer and cut ¼ inch off the fat end. Carrots are a great raw snack, but their sweetness truly comes through when cooked. Very little nutritional value is lost in cooking, unless you overcook them until mushy. In fact, the nutrients in lightly steamed carrots are more usable by your body than those in raw carrots, because cooking breaks down their tough cell walls, releasing beta-carotene.

nutrients per serving:

Carrots
½ cup raw

Calories 25
Protein 1g
Total Fat 0g
Saturated Fat 0g
Cholesterol 0mg
Carbohydrate 6g
Dietary Fiber 2g
Sodium 40mg
Potassium 195mg
Calcium 20mg
Iron 0.2mg
Vitamin A 10,191 IU
Vitamin C 4mg
Folate 12mcg

hearty vegetable stew

1 tablespoon olive oil
1 cup chopped onion
¾ cup chopped carrots
3 cloves garlic, minced
4 cups coarsely chopped green
   cabbage
3½ cups coarsely chopped unpeeled
   new red potatoes
1 teaspoon salt
1 teaspoon dried rosemary
½ teaspoon black pepper
4 cups vegetable broth
1 can (about 15 ounces) Great
   Northern beans, rinsed and
   drained
1 can (about 14 ounces) diced
   tomatoes
   Grated Parmesan cheese (optional)

1. Heat oil in large saucepan over medium-high heat. Add onion and carrots; cook and stir 3 minutes. Add garlic; cook and stir 1 minute.

2. Add cabbage, potatoes, salt, rosemary and pepper; cook 1 minute. Stir in broth, beans and tomatoes; bring to a boil. Reduce heat to medium-low; simmer 15 minutes or until potatoes are tender. Sprinkle with cheese, if desired. *Makes 7 servings*

nutrients per serving:

Calories 220
Calories from Fat 9%
Protein 9g
Carbohydrate 40g
Fiber 9g

Total Fat 3g
Saturated Fat 0g
Cholesterol 0mg
Sodium 590mg

Cauliflower

Pure white cauliflower is a lot more nutritious than it looks. This healthy cruciferous vegetable is versatile enough to blend with and enhance many other flavors. No wonder it is a favorite in cuisines from Italy to India.

benefits

After citrus fruits, cauliflower is your next best natural source of vitamin C, an antioxidant vitamin with wide-ranging effects. Research suggests vitamin C may help defend blood vessels from damage and possibly slow the hardening of arteries that can lead to heart attack or stroke. It may also lower the risk of high blood pressure, arthritis, sight-stealing macular degeneration and asthma. Plus, the natural chemical that gives cauliflower its sharp taste may help protect against cancers of the breast and prostate.

selection and storage

Though cauliflower is available year-round, it's more reasonably priced in fall and winter. Look for creamy white heads with compact florets. Brown patches and opened florets are signs of aging. Store unwashed, uncut cauliflower loosely wrapped in a plastic bag in your refrigerator's crisper drawer. It will keep up to five days.

preparation and serving tips

Remove outer leaves, trim brown spots, break off florets and wash them under running water. Cauliflower serves up well both raw and cooked. Raw, its flavor is less intense and great with a low-fat dip. Steam or microwave cauliflower, but don't overcook it. Try roasting cauliflower tossed in a bit of olive oil to bring out its sweetness. Serve cauliflower plain or with a little dill weed or flavored olive oil. For a low-calorie mock mashed potato dish, mash cooked cauliflower with olive oil, garlic and milk.

nutrients per serving:

Cauliflower ½ cup cooked		
Calories 14	Saturated Fat 0g	Calcium 10mg
Protein 1g	Cholesterol 0mg	Iron 0.2mg
Total Fat 0g	Carbohydrate 3g	Vitamin A 7 IU
	Dietary Fiber 1.5g	Vitamin C 28mg
	Sodium 10mg	Folate 27mcg
	Potassium 90mg	

cauliflower tabbouleh

- 2 packages (12 ounces each) cauliflower florets
- 3 tablespoons olive oil, divided
- 1 teaspoon curry powder
- 1 small bunch Italian parsley
- ½ seedless cucumber, chopped (1½ cups)
- 1 medium onion, finely chopped (¾ cup)
- 1 cup chopped tomato *or* 1 can (about 14 ounces) no-salt-added diced tomatoes, well drained
- ⅓ cup fresh lemon juice
- ½ teaspoon black pepper
- ¼ teaspoon salt
  Romaine lettuce

nutrients per serving:

Calories 114	**Total Fat** 7g
Calories from Fat 52%	**Saturated Fat** <1g
Protein 3g	**Cholesterol** 0mg
Carbohydrate 12g	**Sodium** 141mg
Fiber 4g	

1. Cut large cauliflower florets into uniform pieces. Place cauliflower in food processor; pulse 1 minute or until chopped into uniform granules.

2. Heat 1 tablespoon oil in large nonstick skillet over medium-high heat. Add curry powder; cook until sizzling. Add cauliflower; stir-fry about 10 minutes or until cooked through. Remove from heat and cool.

3. Meanwhile, rinse parsley, trim and discard large stems. Place parsley sprigs in food processor; pulse 10 to 20 seconds to chop.

4. Combine cauliflower mixture, parsley, cucumber, onion and tomato in large bowl. Whisk remaining 2 tablespoons oil, lemon juice, pepper and salt in small bowl. Pour over cauliflower mixture; toss well. Serve at room temperature or chilled on lettuce leaves.

Makes 6 servings

Cheese

Although cheese can be high in fat, a little goes a long way. A sprinkling of Parmesan cheese over a vegetable dish or a snack of fruit accompanied by a bit of Cheddar are indulgences that can also make nutritional sense.

benefits

Cheese is a concentrated source of many of the beneficial nutrients in milk, including calcium. A serving of cheese supplies 20 percent of the recommended daily intake of calcium. Most adults get too little calcium, yet consuming enough is essential for building and maintaining healthy bones and preventing osteoporosis. It may also help reduce the risk of high blood cholesterol, high blood pressure and stroke. Calcium even eases premenstrual symptoms in some women. Eating cheese also helps protect teeth from cavity-causing bacteria, and consuming low-fat dairy products including cheese may aid in weight control.

selection and storage

There are hundreds of varieties of cheese, and many are available in various forms (sliced, cubed, shredded, grated, crumbled, spreadable, etc.). Look for reduced-fat or part-skim varieties to save on calories and fat. Purchase cheese by the "sell by" date and store, tightly wrapped, in the refrigerator's cheese compartment for up to several weeks.

preparation and serving tips

When enjoying cheese as a snack, keep your portion to 1 or 2 ounces. When paired with fruits, vegetables and whole grains, cheese helps boost the flavor of these nutrient-rich foods. Hard cheeses, such as Parmesan or Asiago, and sharp cheeses, such as Cheddar or Gorgonzola, allow you to add intense flavor in small amounts, so you get more delicious cheese flavor for fewer calories.

nutrients per serving:

Cheese, reduced-fat provolone
1 ounce

Calories 77
Protein 7g
Total Fat 5g
Saturated Fat 3g
Cholesterol 15mg
Carbohydrate 1g
Dietary Fiber 0g
Sodium 245mg
Potassium 39mg
Calcium 212mg
Iron 0.2mg
Vitamin A 149 IU
Phosphorus 139mg
Vitamin B12 0.4mcg

nutrients per serving:

Calories 218
Calories from Fat 17%
Protein 14g

Carbohydrate 33g
Fiber 2g
Total Fat 4g
Saturated Fat 2g
Cholesterol 10mg
Sodium 491mg

egg and green chile rice casserole

- ¾ cup uncooked instant brown rice
- ½ cup chopped green onions
- ½ teaspoon ground cumin
- 1 can (4 ounces) chopped mild green chiles, drained
- ⅛ teaspoon salt
- 1 cup cholesterol-free egg substitute
- ½ cup (2 ounces) shredded reduced-fat sharp Cheddar cheese or Mexican cheese blend
- ¼ cup pico de gallo
- 1 medium lime, quartered

1. Preheat oven to 350°F. Lightly coat 8-inch square baking dish with nonstick cooking spray.

2. Cook rice according to package directions. Remove from heat; stir in green onions and cumin. Transfer to prepared baking dish.

3. Sprinkle chiles and salt evenly over rice mixture. Pour egg substitute evenly over top. Bake 30 to 35 minutes or until center is set.

4. Sprinkle with cheese. Bake 3 minutes or until cheese is melted. Let stand 5 minutes. Serve with pico de gallo and lime wedges.

Makes 4 servings

Cherries

Whether sweet or tart, dried or juiced, fresh, frozen or canned, cherries pack a powerful nutritional punch in a small package of flavor. Sweet cherries make an ideal snack or dessert. Tart cherries offer some important health benefits and work well in savory as well as sweet dishes.

nutrients per serving:

Cherries, sweet, fresh ½ cup

Calories 49
Protein 1g
Total Fat 0g
Saturated Fat 0g
Cholesterol 0mg
Carbohydrate 12g
Dietary Fiber 2g
Sodium 0mg
Potassium 170mg
Calcium 10mg
Iron 0.3mg
Vitamin A 49 IU
Vitamin C 5mg
Folate 3mcg

benefits

Emerging evidence links cherries to important health benefits, from helping to ease the pain of arthritis and gout to reducing risk factors for heart disease, diabetes and certain cancers. Compared to sweet cherries, tart (or sour) cherries are higher in vitamins and minerals, but both types provide disease-fighting antioxidants, including beta-carotene and vitamin C. Cherries supply potassium, which is essential for healthy blood pressure, and soluble fiber, which helps lower cholesterol and regulate blood sugar. Cherries also contain melatonin, which has been found to help regulate the body's natural sleep patterns and aid with jet lag. It may even play a role in preventing memory loss and delaying the aging process.

selection and storage

Most fresh cherries are available from May through August. Choose brightly colored, shiny and plump cherries without blemishes. Store unwashed cherries in a plastic bag in the refrigerator. Cherries with stems tend to last longer, but plan to use any cherries within a few days. Dried cherries are available in sweet and sour varieties but may contain added sugar.

preparation and serving tips

Sweet cherries are best when eaten fresh. For a sweet addition to salads, toss in dried or fresh sweet cherries. Most tart cherries are too sour to eat raw but make excellent sauces, pies, relishes and preserves.

cherry & mushroom stuffed pork chops

- 2 tablespoons vegetable oil, divided
- 1 cup chopped fresh shiitake mushrooms
- ¼ cup finely chopped onion
- ¼ cup finely chopped celery
- ¼ cup sweetened dried cherries, chopped
- ¼ teaspoon salt
- ⅛ teaspoon dried thyme
- ⅛ teaspoon black pepper
- 4 boneless pork loin chops (about 1¼ pounds), cut 1 inch thick
- 1 teaspoon all-purpose flour
- ¼ cup fat-free reduced-sodium chicken broth
- ¼ cup cherry juice

1. Heat 1 tablespoon oil in large skillet over medium-high heat. Add mushrooms, onion and celery; cook and stir 4 minutes. Stir in cherries, salt, thyme and pepper. Remove from heat.

2. Make deep pocket in side of each pork chop; fill with one fourth of cherry stuffing. Skewer pockets closed with toothpicks.

3. Heat remaining 1 tablespoon oil in same skillet over medium heat. Add pork chops. Brown 7 to 8 minutes per side or until cooked through.

4. Remove pork from skillet. Pour off fat. Add flour to skillet; cook 30 seconds, stirring constantly. Stir in broth and juice, scraping up browned bits from bottom of skillet. Cook 1 minute to thicken sauce slightly.

5. Return pork chops to skillet and turn to coat evenly. Serve pork with sauce.

Makes 4 servings

nutrients per serving:

Calories 275
Calories from Fat 32%
Protein 28g
Carbohydrate 19g
Fiber 1g
Total Fat 10g
Saturated Fat 2g
Cholesterol 65mg
Sodium 394mg

Chicken Breast

Chicken breast is one of the leanest, most versatile meats you'll find. It's a delicious source of high quality protein with less saturated fat than other meats.

benefits

Whether a diet is designed to prevent heart attacks, decrease cancer risk, manage diabetes, lower blood pressure or reduce cholesterol, it's likely to include chicken breast. That's because an important part of fighting these potential killers is limiting saturated and total fat, cholesterol and calories while getting essential nutrients. Skinless chicken breast, prepared and served in a healthy manner, fits the bill better than most other sources of complete protein.

selection and storage

Chicken breasts are available in various forms. Whole breasts with the skin on are the most economical. For convenience, boneless, skinless chicken breasts are another option, but if they are preseasoned, they can be high in sodium. Refrigerate raw chicken for up to two days, cooked chicken up to three days. When freezing raw chicken, seal tightly in a plastic bag to prevent freezer burn. Use frozen chicken within two months.

preparation and serving tips

To help chicken breast retain its lean profile, use a low-fat cooking method such as baking, roasting, grilling, broiling or stewing. Remove the skin to cut the fat in half. It makes little nutritional difference whether the skin is removed before or after cooking, but the meat is more moist and tender when cooked skin on. Cook chicken until the internal temperature is 165°F. Boneless chicken will cook faster than its bone-in counterpart, just avoid overcooking, which will make it dry and tough.

nutrients per serving:

**Chicken Breast, skinless
3 ounces roasted**

Calories 140
Protein 26g
Total Fat 3g
Saturated Fat 1g
Cholesterol 72mg
Carbohydrate 0g
Dietary Fiber 0g
Sodium 60mg
Potassium 220mg
Iron 0.9mg
Vitamin B6 0.5mg
Vitamin B12 0.3mcg
Niacin 12mcg

chicken piccata

- 3 tablespoons all-purpose flour
- ½ teaspoon salt
- ¼ teaspoon black pepper
- 4 boneless skinless chicken breasts (4 ounces each)
- 2 teaspoons olive oil
- 1 teaspoon butter
- 2 cloves garlic, minced
- ¾ cup fat-free reduced-sodium chicken broth
- 1 tablespoon fresh lemon juice
- 2 tablespoons chopped fresh Italian parsley
- 1 tablespoon capers, drained

1. Combine flour, salt and pepper in shallow dish. Reserve 1 tablespoon flour mixture.

2. Pound chicken between waxed paper to ½-inch thickness with flat side of meat mallet or rolling pin. Coat chicken with remaining flour mixture, shaking off excess.

3. Heat oil and butter in large nonstick skillet over medium heat. Add chicken; cook 4 to 5 minutes per side or until no longer pink in center. Transfer to serving platter; cover loosely with foil.

4. Add garlic to same skillet; cook and stir 1 minute. Add reserved 1 tablespoon flour mixture; cook and stir 1 minute. Add broth and lemon juice; cook 2 minutes or until thickened, stirring frequently. Stir in parsley and capers; spoon sauce over chicken.

Makes 4 servings

nutrients per serving:

Calories 194
Calories from Fat 30%
Protein 27g
Carbohydrate 5g
Fiber <1g
Total Fat 6g
Saturated Fat 2g
Cholesterol 71mg
Sodium 473mg

Cinnamon

The sweet warmth of cinnamon has been appreciated for centuries. It has been used as everything from a love potion to the cure for an upset tummy. Perhaps we shouldn't be surprised that cinnamon holds promise in supporting overall health and wellness.

benefits

Warming your diet with cinnamon feeds your immune system with antioxidant fuel for the fight against infection and disease. Cinnamon has one of the highest antioxidant levels of any spice; it even has more than many foods. You'll get as many antioxidants from 1 teaspoon of cinnamon as from ½ cup of blueberries. And according to several studies, a mere ½ teaspoon of cinnamon daily can improve insulin sensitivity, which in turn can help lower diabetes and heart disease risk. Cinnamon may also relieve bloating and gas and reduce heartburn discomfort.

selection and storage

Cinnamon is available ground or as sticks, or scrolls, of dried bark. Ground cinnamon has a stronger flavor than the sticks and can stay fresh for six months, while the scrolls last longer. Both should be stored in a cool, dark, dry place.

preparation and serving tips

Cinnamon adds a warm, distinctive flavor to both sweet and savory dishes. Often paired with apples and added to sweet baked goods, cinnamon also brings sweetness and flavor to Middle Eastern and Asian recipes. In fact, cinnamon is an ingredient in curry powder. Be adventurous with cinnamon—the possibilities are endless. Perk up drinks such as coffee, tea, smoothies or mulled wine with sticks of cinnamon. Sprinkle cinnamon on cereal, ice cream, pudding or yogurt. Add cinnamon to marinades for lamb or beef.

nutrients per serving:

Cinnamon, ground 1 teaspoon		
Calories 6	Total Fat 0g	Potassium 11mg
Protein 0g	Saturated Fat 0g	Calcium 26mg
	Cholesterol 0mg	Iron 0.2mg
	Carbohydrate 2g	Vitamin A 8 IU
	Dietary Fiber 1g	
	Sodium 0mg	

cinnamon caramel corn

8 cups air-popped popcorn
   (about ⅓ cup kernels)
2 tablespoons honey
4 teaspoons butter
¼ teaspoon ground cinnamon

nutrients per serving:

Calories 117	**Total Fat** 4g
Calories from Fat 29%	**Saturated Fat** 1g
Protein 2g	**Cholesterol** 0mg
Carbohydrate 19g	**Sodium** 45mg
Fiber 1g	

1. Preheat oven to 350°F. Spray jelly-roll pan with nonstick cooking spray. Place popcorn in large bowl.

2. Combine honey, butter and cinnamon in small saucepan; cook and stir over low heat until butter is melted and mixture is smooth. Immediately pour over popcorn; toss to coat evenly. Pour onto prepared pan.

3. Bake 12 to 14 minutes or until coating is golden brown and appears crackled, stirring twice.

4. Cool popcorn on pan. (As popcorn cools, coating becomes crisp. If not crisp enough, or if popcorn softens upon standing, return to oven and heat 5 to 8 minutes.) Store in airtight container.   *Makes 4 servings*

Cajun Popcorn: Replace cinnamon with 1 teaspoon Cajun or Creole seasoning and add 1 extra teaspoon honey.

Italian Popcorn: Spray 8 cups air-popped popcorn with fat-free butter-flavored cooking spray to coat. Sprinkle with 2 tablespoons grated Parmesan cheese, ½ teaspoon dried oregano and ⅛ teaspoon black pepper. Gently toss to coat. Bake as directed.

Cocoa

Cocoa powder is made by removing most of the fat (cocoa butter) from the tropical cocoa bean. That leaves rich, sugar-free chocolate flavor that's ready to use in all sorts of guilt-free homemade treats.

benefits

Cocoa powder is packed with natural plant nutrients called flavanols. Recent research indicates flavanols can have beneficial effects on blood pressure and the health of blood vessels, as well as on the body's sensitivity to insulin— all of which help lower the risks of heart attack, stroke and diabetes. Cocoa powder is also nutrient rich—providing fiber and minerals essential for good health, such as iron, magnesium, phosphorus, potassium and copper—yet very low in fat and calories.

selection and storage

Natural cocoa powder is a light brown color and more acidic than Dutch process cocoa, which is a darker reddish brown. It's best to choose the type the recipe calls for since the lower acidity of Dutch process cocoa can change performance, especially in cakes and cookies. Keep cocoa powder in an opaque, airtight container in a cool, dark place; it will last up to two years. Don't mistake cocoa powder for hot cocoa mix, which blends cocoa powder with powdered milk and sugar, resulting in a different product.

preparation and serving tips

Cocoa powder is most often used in baked goods, such as brownies and cakes, and can also be used in puddings and beverages. Cocoa powder has savory abilities, too, as in classic Mexican moles or as the "secret" ingredient in homemade chili recipes. When natural cocoa (an acid) is used in recipes calling for baking soda (an alkali), it creates a leavening action that causes the batter to rise in the oven. Dutch process cocoa needs baking powder to create the same effect.

nutrients per serving:

**Cocoa Powder
1 tablespoon**

Calories 12
Protein 1g
Total Fat 0.5g
Saturated Fat 0g
Cholesterol 0mg
Carbohydrate 3g
Dietary Fiber 2g
Sodium 0mg
Potassium 82mg
Calcium 7mg
Iron 0.8mg
Magnesium 27mg
Phosphorus 40mg
Copper 0.2mg

raspberry-glazed brownies with cheesecake topping

- ¾ cup all-purpose flour
- 9 tablespoons sucralose-sugar blend, divided
- ¼ cup unsweetened cocoa powder
- ¾ teaspoon baking powder
- ⅛ teaspoon salt
- 1 jar (2½ ounces) baby food prunes
- ¼ cup cold coffee or fat-free (skim) milk
- 1 egg
- 2 tablespoons canola oil
- ¾ teaspoon vanilla, divided
- ¼ cup seedless raspberry fruit spread
- 2 ounces reduced-fat cream cheese, softened
- 4½ teaspoons fat-free (skim) milk

1. Preheat oven to 350°F.

2. Combine flour, 7 tablespoons sucralose-sugar blend, cocoa, baking powder and salt in large bowl; stir until well blended. Combine prunes, coffee, egg, oil and ½ teaspoon vanilla in medium bowl; stir until well blended.

3. Make well in center of dry ingredients; add prune mixture. Stir just until blended.

4. Spread batter evenly in ungreased 8×8-inch nonstick baking pan. Bake 8 minutes. (Brownies will not appear to be done.) Cool completely in pan on wire rack.

5. Meanwhile, place raspberry spread in small microwavable bowl. Microwave on HIGH 10 seconds; stir until smooth. Brush evenly over brownies with pastry brush.

6. Combine cream cheese, 4½ teaspoons milk, remaining 2 tablespoons sucralose-sugar blend and ¼ teaspoon vanilla in medium bowl. Beat with electric mixer at medium speed until well blended and smooth. To serve, top each brownie with 1 teaspoon cream cheese mixture.

Makes 12 servings

nutrients per serving:

Calories 143
Calories from Fat 24%
Protein 2g

Carbohydrate 24g
Fiber 1g
Total Fat 4g
Saturated Fat 1g
Cholesterol 20mg
Sodium 85mg

Coffee

The caffeine buzz that coffee provides not only helps us face the morning, it offers other potential health benefits, too. Without added cream, sugar and toppings, coffee is carb free, cholesterol free, fat free and almost calorie free, so drink up!

benefits

Coffee was once cast as a health villain, but fortunately for java fans, more recent research indicates the opposite is true. In various studies, coffee consumption has been linked with lower rates of Parkinson's disease, gallstones, type 2 diabetes, liver cancer, heart arrhythmias, stroke (in women) and even Alzheimer's disease. While caffeine may be behind some of these positive effects, researchers point to coffee's anti-inflammatory action, its hefty dose of protective antioxidants and its ability to lessen insulin resistance as potential sources of coffee's health benefits.

selection and storage

You'll find many coffee selections in the grocery store—from whole to ground, mild- to full-bodied, caffeinated to decaffeinated and instant to flavored. Choose the form and flavor depending on how you plan to prepare it and on your taste preference. Store coffee beans or ground coffee in an airtight container in a cool, dry place. If you won't use the beans within a week or ground coffee within a few days, keep the coffee in the freezer.

preparation and serving tips

Roasted coffee beans are ground and brewed to create the coffee we love. But beware of coffee drinks loaded with sugar, syrups, whole milk, flavorings and whipped toppings, which can add loads of calories and fat. Coffee is a natural companion to chocolate in desserts and can add subtle depth in recipes for chili, pasta sauce and gravy or in glazes for meats.

nutrients per serving:

Coffee 1 cup brewed		
Calories 2	**Saturated Fat** 0g	**Potassium** 116mg
Protein 0g	**Cholesterol** 0mg	**Magnesium** 7mg
Total Fat 0g	**Carbohydrate** 0g	**Calcium** 5mg
	Dietary Fiber 0g	**Folate** 5mcg
	Sodium 5mg	

light latte cookies

- 1¾ cups all-purpose flour
- ¼ cup unsweetened cocoa powder
- 1 tablespoon instant coffee granules
- 1 teaspoon baking soda
- ½ teaspoon ground cinnamon
- ½ cup (1 stick) soft baking butter with canola oil
- ½ cup packed dark brown sugar
- ¼ cup fat-free sour cream
- 1 egg
- 1 egg white
- 1 teaspoon vanilla
  Powdered sugar (optional)
- ¼ cup chopped bittersweet chocolate
- 2 tablespoons fat-free half-and-half

1. Preheat oven to 350°F. Combine flour, cocoa, coffee, baking soda and cinnamon in large bowl; set aside.

2. Beat butter in large bowl with electric mixer at medium speed 30 seconds or until creamy. Beat in brown sugar and sour cream at medium-low speed until well blended. Add egg, egg white and vanilla; beat at low speed until well blended.

3. Gradually add flour mixture to butter mixture, beating at low speed until well blended.

4. Drop dough by level teaspoonfuls onto ungreased cookie sheets. Flatten cookies slightly with bottom of greased glass. Bake 6 minutes. Cool on cookie sheets 5 minutes. Remove to wire racks; cool completely.

5. Dust cookies with powdered sugar, if desired. For icing, heat chocolate and half-and-half in small saucepan over very low heat, stirring until chocolate melts. Drizzle over cookies. Let stand until icing is firm.

Makes 6 dozen cookies

nutrients per serving:

Calories 66
Calories from Fat 37%
Protein <1g
Carbohydrate 10g
Fiber <1g
Total Fat 2g
Saturated Fat <1g
Cholesterol 6mg
Sodium 76mg

Corn

Nourishing corn is a grain native to America that was central to the survival of the earliest settlers. The golden goodness of corn can be enjoyed in countless ways—corn on the cob, popcorn, corn bread, corn tortillas and corn pudding are just a few.

nutrients per serving:

Corn
½ cup cooked

Calories 72
Protein 3g
Total Fat 1g
Saturated Fat 0g
Cholesterol 0mg
Carbohydrate 16g
Dietary Fiber 2g
Sodium 0mg
Potassium 160mg
Calcium 2mg
Iron 0.3mg
Vitamin A 196 IU
Vitamin C 4mg
Folate 17mcg

benefits

Corn's insoluble fiber helps prevent and treat common digestive ailments such as constipation and hemorrhoids by absorbing water as it travels through the digestive tract. Corn is also a good source of folate, a B vitamin known to support heart health and help prevent birth defects. And corn supplies lutein, a powerful antioxidant that may help reduce the risk of macular degeneration, a primary cause of blindness in older adults.

selection and storage

Once corn is picked, the natural sugar begins turning to starch and it loses some sweetness, so sweet corn is best eaten within a day or two of picking. Once home, refrigerate unhusked corn immediately. Frozen or canned corn kernels preserve much of the flavor and nutrition of fresh. Look for whole grain stone-ground cornmeal rather than the more processed, less nutritious kinds. Buy popcorn kernels to pop yourself, or look for microwave popcorn without extra fat and additives.

preparation and serving tips

Boiling is the traditional method for preparing corn on the cob, though grilling, steaming or even microwaving will get the job done. Overcooking toughens kernels, so cook for the shortest amount of time possible, just a few minutes. Corn makes a sunny addition to salads, soups and casseroles and takes to all kinds of seasonings. For a southwestern flavor, try adding hot peppers or chili powder and a squeeze of lime. Fresh dill or basil pair well with corn, too.

festive corn casserole

2 cups grated zucchini
1 cup frozen corn
1 cup diced red bell pepper
2 cups cholesterol-free egg substitute
½ cup evaporated fat-free milk
2 teaspoons sugar substitute
¼ teaspoon celery seed
⅛ teaspoon salt
⅛ teaspoon red pepper flakes (optional)

1. Preheat oven to 350°F. Coat 11×7-inch baking dish with nonstick cooking spray.

2. Combine zucchini, corn and bell pepper in prepared baking dish. Whisk egg substitute, evaporated milk, sugar substitute, celery seed, salt and red pepper flakes, if desired, in large bowl. Pour egg mixture over vegetables.

3. Bake 45 to 55 minutes or until golden.

Makes 10 servings

nutrients per serving:

Calories 54	**Carbohydrate** 7g	**Saturated Fat** 0g
Calories from Fat <1%	**Fiber** 1g	**Cholesterol** <1mg
Protein 6g	**Total Fat** <1g	**Sodium** 138mg

Cranberries

Cranberries make a colorful and festive addition to holiday tables, but their refreshingly tart taste and amazing health benefits can and should be enjoyed year-round.

benefits

Cranberries contain phytonutrients that prevent certain bacteria from sticking to the walls of the urinary tract, thus helping to prevent or treat urinary tract infections and interstitial cystitis (a condition resulting in bladder and pelvic discomfort). This same antibacterial effect may also help prevent gum disease and stomach ulcers, both commonly caused by bacteria. In addition, cranberries contain fiber as well as significant amounts of antioxidants and other phytonutrients that may help protect against heart disease, cancer and eye diseases.

selection and storage

Fresh cranberries are at their peak from October to December. Choose bags of fresh cranberries that are firm, brightly colored and not shriveled. They can be refrigerated, tightly wrapped, for at least two months or frozen for up to a year. Cranberry juice drinks should be selected with the least amount of added sugar to keep calories in check. Because the pure juice is so tart, cranberry juice blends offer a 100 percent juice option without added sugar. Sweetened dried cranberries are also a good addition to your pantry.

preparation and serving tips

Besides the traditional cranberry relish, this tart fruit can also be baked into pies, cobblers and quick breads or used in chutneys and salsas to complement poultry and pork dishes. Dried cranberries add sweetness and chewiness to salads, cereals and cookies. Or simply enjoy them as a snack in trail mix. Use cranberry juice blends to add intense flavor to healthy smoothie recipes.

nutrients per serving:

Cranberries, dried, sweetened ¼ cup		
Calories 99		
Protein 0g		Dietary Fiber 2g
Total Fat 0g		Sodium 0mg
Saturated Fat 0g		Potassium 15mg
Cholesterol 0mg		Calcium 3mg
Carbohydrate 26g		Iron 0.2mg

Currants

These dried Zante grapes look like tiny raisins, but they're more concentrated in flavor and nutrients than raisins are. Use them as you would raisins to add sweetness to baked goods, cereals and trail mix.

benefits

Currants supply a healthy helping of dietary fiber, and because that fiber is a mix of both soluble and insoluble, it benefits health on multiple fronts. Insoluble fiber helps to prevent and relieve constipation, while soluble fiber helps decrease blood pressure and blood cholesterol levels, lowering your risk of heart disease and stroke. Currants are also one of the top food sources of the trace mineral boron. Studies have shown that boron may provide protection against osteoporosis and possibly mimic the positive effects of estrogen replacement therapy (ERT) in postmenopausal women, but without ERT's risks. Currants are also loaded with potassium, a mineral that helps keep body fluids in balance and, along with magnesium and calcium, keeps blood pressure in check.

selection and storage

Zante currants are available in supermarkets next to the other dried fruits and raisins. They should be stored in a dry, cool place. Once opened, they should be tightly sealed to prevent them from drying out and used within about three months.

preparation and serving tips

Currants offer tiny bursts of sweetness when added to different foods. Try sprinkling them on cereal or yogurt or adding them to chicken or tuna salad. Add them to cookies, muffins or quick breads. They can be added to rice dishes or mixed into stuffing. They also work well in baked fruit desserts, such as apple crisp.

nutrients per serving:

**Zante Currants
¼ cup**

Calories 102
Protein 1.5g
Total Fat 0g
Saturated Fat 0g
Cholesterol 0mg
Carbohydrate 27g
Dietary Fiber 2.5g
Sodium 3mg
Potassium 321mg
Calcium 31mg
Iron 1.2mg
Magnesium 15mg
Vitamin C 2mg

Curry

What we call curry powder is actually a mix of as many as 20 different spices used in Indian cooking. The blend usually includes turmeric, coriander, cumin, fennel seed, cardamom, nutmeg, black pepper, chiles and more. There are as many variations as there are cooks in India.

nutrients per serving:

**Curry Powder
1 teaspoon**

Calories 6
Protein 0g
Total Fat 0g
Saturated Fat 0g
Cholesterol 0mg
Carbohydrate 1g
Dietary Fiber 0.5g
Sodium 0mg
Potassium 30mg
Calcium 10mg
Iron 0.6mg
Vitamin A 20 IU
Folate 3mcg

benefits

The healing benefits of the individual ingredients in curry powder combine to give it its "super" powers. Turmeric, for example, gives curries their characteristic yellow color, and research suggests this spice—and its active ingredient, curcumin—can aid digestion and help relieve bloating and gas. Cumin, coriander and fennel remedy digestive discomforts, too. Research also indicates that turmeric and other antioxidant-rich curry powder ingredients may help reduce inflammation and prevent the buildup of plaque and blood clots within arteries that can cause a heart attack or stroke.

selection and storage

The best curry powder is one you make fresh yourself by toasting and grinding together the various spices. But if you don't have the time, there are plenty of choices of prepared curry powder available—some are spicy, some mild and almost sweet with cinnamon and nutmeg. Try a few and you'll find a favorite. Garam masala is a mild, sweet curry powder. Madras curry powder has more heat. Whatever you choose, store it in a cool, dry place and use it up in two to three months before the complex flavor and aroma fade away.

preparation and serving tips

Although Indian cooking is what first comes to mind, Caribbean, Asian and even Japanese cuisines have their own versions of curry powder. There's no need to limit its use to traditional dishes, either. Curry powder can perk up vegetables of all kinds, from potatoes to broccoli (after all, it originated in a country that is largely vegetarian). It can even add an exotic touch to stews, casseroles or burgers.

curried eggplant, squash & chickpea stew

- 1 teaspoon olive oil
- ½ cup diced red bell pepper
- ¼ cup diced onion
- 1¼ teaspoons curry powder
- 1 clove garlic, minced
- ½ teaspoon salt
- 1¼ cups cubed peeled eggplant
- ¾ cup cubed peeled acorn or butternut squash
- ⅔ cup rinsed and drained canned chickpeas
- ½ cup water
- 3 tablespoons white wine
  Hot pepper sauce (optional)
- ¼ cup lemon yogurt (optional)
- 2 tablespoons chopped fresh parsley (optional)

1. Heat oil in medium saucepan over medium heat. Add bell pepper and onion; cook and stir 5 minutes. Add curry powder, garlic and salt; cook and stir 1 minute. Add eggplant, squash, chickpeas, water and wine. Cover; bring to a boil. Reduce heat and simmer 20 to 25 minutes or just until squash and eggplant are tender.

2. Season to taste with hot pepper sauce, if desired. Serve with yogurt and parsley, if desired.   *Makes 2 servings*

nutrients per serving:

Calories 180
Calories from Fat 30%
Protein 5g
Carbohydrate 26g

Fiber 7g
Total Fat 6g
Saturated Fat <1g
Cholesterol 0mg
Sodium 780mg

Dark Chocolate

Chocolate lovers, rejoice! Dark chocolate tastes sinfully delicious, but it comes with some important health benefits. Indulge in moderation and choose real dark chocolate with a high cocoa content instead of milk chocolate candy bars.

benefits

Packed with natural antioxidants, essential minerals and protective plant nutrients called flavanols, dark chocolate may protect heart health by lowering blood pressure and preventing blockages in the arteries that feed the heart. Dark chocolate does contain saturated fat—which tends to raise blood cholesterol levels and heart disease risk—but it's a unique form called stearic acid that doesn't negatively affect blood cholesterol. Still, most of dark chocolate's benefits are associated with only moderate consumption— 1 or 2 ounces per week. It's high in fat and calories, so eating too much can cause weight gain that increases your risk of several serious diseases.

selection and storage

Dark chocolate includes semisweet and bittersweet and is often labeled with the percent of cocoa. This refers to the percent of ingredients derived from the cocoa bean. In chocolate with 60 percent cocoa, the remaining 40 percent is some combination of sugar, vanilla and other ingredients. The higher the percentage of cocoa, the more intense and bitter the flavor will be. Store dark chocolate tightly wrapped in a cool, dry place; warmer temperatures can cause grayish streaks, which do not affect flavor. Under ideal conditions, it can be stored for years without losing quality.

preparation and serving tips

Dark chocolate is a delicacy that is best enjoyed on its own in small amounts. It can also be used in baking, in a wide variety of desserts or simply as a garnish for a healthy dessert.

nutrients per serving:

**Dark Chocolate
1 ounce**

Calories 154
Protein 1g
Total Fat 9g
Saturated Fat 5g
Cholesterol 2mg
Carbohydrate 17g
Dietary Fiber 2g
Sodium 6mg
Potassium 160mg
Calcium 16mg
Iron 2.3mg
Magnesium 43mg
Copper 0.3mg
Phosphorus 60mg

mystical layered bars

- ⅓ cup (⅔ stick) butter
- 1 cup graham cracker crumbs
- ½ cup old-fashioned or quick oats
- 1 can (14 ounces) sweetened condensed milk
- 1 cup flaked coconut
- ¾ cup semisweet chocolate chips
- ¾ cup raisins
- 1 cup coarsely chopped pecans

1. Preheat oven to 350°F. Melt butter in 13×9-inch baking pan. Remove from oven. Spread butter evenly in pan.

2. Sprinkle graham cracker crumbs and oats evenly over butter; press with fork. Drizzle condensed milk over crust. Layer coconut, chocolate chips, raisins and pecans over milk.

3. Bake 25 to 30 minutes or until lightly browned. Cool 5 minutes; cut into 2×1½-inch bars. Cool completely in pan on wire rack. Store tightly covered at room temperature.

Makes 2 dozen bars

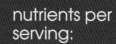

nutrients per serving:

Calories 180
Calories from Fat 51%
Protein 3g
Carbohydrate 22g
Fiber 2g
Total Fat 10g
Saturated Fat 5g
Cholesterol 10mg
Sodium 70mg

73

Dates

Dates grow in clusters on tall, stately date palm trees, which flourish in California, Arizona and the Middle East. Their concentrated sweetness comes with a big helping of fiber and nutrition.

benefits

Despite their small size and sweet taste, dates are loaded with insoluble and soluble fiber, so they can play a part in getting and keeping your digestive system running smoothly, lowering LDL ("bad") and total cholesterol levels and treating high blood pressure. Their soluble fiber may help improve the body's response to insulin, too. Dates are also high in potassium, and research indicates that eating lots of potassium-rich foods can cut the risk of stroke and heart disease.

selection and storage

Dates are dried, so their skins are somewhat wrinkled like raisins. There are many varieties, from very soft and plump to small and dry. For eating out of hand, it's hard to beat the large, soft Medjool, which is available in the fall. Packaged dates come pitted, unpitted or chopped. Drier dates, like the Deglet Noor, the most common variety in the United States, keep for up to a year well wrapped in the refrigerator. Softer dates should also be refrigerated but have a shorter period of freshness.

preparation and serving tips

Dates are great on their own, but for a real treat, try stuffing them with nuts, such as whole almonds or chopped walnuts or pecans. For a spicy twist, tuck in a piece of crystallized ginger. Adding dates to home-baked breads, cakes, muffins and cookies adds richness and nutrition to recipes. Dates also work well in fruit compotes, salads and desserts. Chopped or slivered, dates can also top rice, couscous or vegetable dishes. To slice or chop dates, chill them first. The colder they are, the easier they are to slice.

nutrients per serving:

Dates, dried
¼ cup

Calories 104
Protein 1g
Total Fat 0g
Saturated Fat 0g
Cholesterol 0mg
Carbohydrate 28g
Dietary Fiber 3g
Sodium 0mg
Potassium 240mg
Calcium 14mg
Iron 0.4mg
Vitamin A 4 IU
B₆ 0.1mg
Folate 7mcg
Niacin 0.5mg

Edamame

Edamame (pronounced eh-dah-MAH-meh) are fresh green soybeans. Squeezed out of the pod, edamame are a favorite Japanese bar snack. Shelled edamame make a high protein substitute for other beans or legumes.

benefits

Even other legumes have trouble stacking up to edamame. These little wonders provide complete protein—protein that includes all the amino acids the body requires but is almost exclusively found in animal products, which tend to be higher in saturated fats and calories. And soy protein contains isoflavones, a phytonutrient associated with healthy cholesterol levels that may also help protect against cancer, high blood pressure and osteoporosis. Edamame also provide essential omega-3 fats that research says can reduce inflammation and may help prevent certain causes of blindness and lower the risk of chronic diseases such as arthritis, heart disease and cancer.

selection and storage

Edamame, in the pods or already shelled, are available in the frozen vegetable section. Frozen edamame may be stored for at least six months. Fresh edamame are occasionally available in the produce section of ethnic markets.

preparation and serving tips

To cook edamame, boil, steam, sauté or microwave. Check package directions and don't overcook. The beans should be tender but firm. You can enjoy edamame directly from the pod as a snack or appetizer.

In Japan, the beans are squeezed out of the pods with the teeth. (The tough pods are always discarded.) You can add the shelled beans to soups, stews, salads and pasta or rice dishes for added fiber and protein.

nutrients per serving:

**Edamame, shelled
½ cup cooked**

Calories 95
Protein 8g
Total Fat 4g
Saturated Fat 0.5g
Cholesterol 0mg
Carbohydrate 8g
Dietary Fiber 4g
Sodium 5mg
Potassium 340mg
Calcium 49mg
Iron 1.7mg
Vitamin C 5mg
Folate 241mcg

Eggs

Eggs are a near-perfect food loaded with vitamins and protein. No wonder they have symbolized fertility, creation and rebirth in story and myth across cultures since ancient times.

benefits

Eggs are one of nature's most economical nutrient packages—complete with 13 essential vitamins and minerals, high-quality protein, healthy unsaturated fats and protective antioxidants— all for about 75 calories. Eggs provide a third to half of the daily need for choline, a vitamin essential for brain development in fetuses and infants that may also help prevent age-related memory loss and promote liver and heart health. Eggs are a good source of the antioxidants lutein and zeaxanthin that, according to many studies, reduce the risk of sight-stealing cataracts and macular degeneration in older adults. Although eggs are high in cholesterol, they're fairly low in fat, and evidence consistently shows that eating one or more eggs each day does not increase heart disease risk in healthy adults and may actually be associated with lower blood pressure.

selection and storage

Choose eggs that are clean and crack-free and check the "sell-by" date. Brown eggs are no more nutritious than white; neither are those labeled "free-range" or "cage-free." Fresher eggs hold their shapes better when poached or fried, but older eggs are easier to peel when hard cooked. Store eggs in their original carton in the coldest part of the refrigerator, not in the door. Use within three weeks.

preparation and serving tips

Even on their own, eggs are amazingly versatile. They can be scrambled, poached, coddled, whipped into a soufflé or hard cooked for a salad. For safety sake, if you are using eggs in a custard or other similar recipe, heat the egg mixture to 160°F for a few seconds to destroy any harmful bacteria.

nutrients per serving:

Egg
1 large boiled

Calories 78
Protein 6g
Total Fat 5g
Saturated Fat 2g
Cholesterol 186mg
Carbohydrate <1g
Dietary Fiber 0g
Sodium 60mg
Potassium 65mg
Calcium 25mg
Iron 0.6mg
Vitamin A 260 IU
Vitamin D 44 IU
Choline 113mg

light-style breakfast sandwiches

4 **eggs**
¼ **teaspoon salt (optional)**
¼ **teaspoon black pepper** *or* ⅛ **teaspoon hot pepper sauce**
3 **slices (2 ounces) Canadian bacon, chopped**
1 **green onion, thinly sliced**
2 **teaspoons butter**
⅓ **cup shredded reduced-fat sharp Cheddar cheese**
4 **multigrain or whole wheat English muffins, split and toasted**

1. Beat eggs, salt, if desired, and pepper in medium bowl. Stir in bacon and green onion.

2. Heat butter in medium nonstick skillet over medium-high heat until bubbly. Add egg mixture; cook, stirring frequently, 2 to 3 minutes or until eggs are soft-set. Remove from heat; stir in cheese. Serve on English muffins. *Makes 4 servings*

Figs

The fig tree is an ancient symbol of abundance, fertility and sweetness. Fresh or dried, figs add delightful flavor to everything from cookies to savory sauces.

benefits

Figs are a rich source of potassium, which is essential for controlling blood pressure. They also provide calcium, a mineral many Americans don't get enough of that is necessary for preventing osteoporosis, and iron, which carries oxygen to all the cells of the body. Compared to other fresh and dried fruits, figs are higher in fiber, especially the soluble variety that helps lower blood cholesterol. They also add valuable nutrients to the diet to help fight off many common diseases.

selection and storage

Fresh figs are available only for a short time after they are harvested in late summer or early fall. Choose ones that are plump, tender, free from bruises and firm to the touch. Ripe figs should not be washed until ready to eat and should be kept covered and refrigerated, where they will remain fresh for only a day or two. Dried and canned figs are available year-round; dried figs can be stored for six to eight months.

preparation and serving tips

To eat a fresh fig, there is no need to peel—just snip off the stem and enjoy. Chopped or sliced figs add rich sweetness to salads and hot or cold cereals. Fresh and dried figs can be used in baked goods, jams, jellies and preserves. Fresh figs make easy and elegant hors d'oeuvres wrapped in a slice of prosciutto or stuffed with a bit of goat cheese. Figs also pair well with meats, such as lamb, veal and poultry.

nutrients per serving:

Figs, dried
¼ cup

Calories 93
Protein 1g
Total Fat 0g
Saturated Fat 0g
Cholesterol 0mg
Carbohydrate 24g
Dietary Fiber 3.5g
Sodium 0mg
Potassium 250mg
Calcium 60mg
Iron 0.8mg
Vitamin A 4 IU
Folate 3mcg

fig bars

Filling

- ½ cup dried figs
- 6 tablespoons hot water
- 1 tablespoon granulated sugar

Dough

- ⅔ cup all-purpose flour
- ½ cup quick oats
- ¾ teaspoon baking powder
- ¼ teaspoon salt
- 2 tablespoons vegetable oil
- 3 tablespoons fat-free (skim) milk

Icing

- 1 ounce reduced-fat cream cheese, softened
- ⅓ cup powdered sugar
- ½ teaspoon vanilla

1. Preheat oven to 400°F. Spray cookie sheet with nonstick cooking spray.

2. Combine figs, water and granulated sugar in food processor or blender; process until figs are finely chopped. Set aside.

3. Combine flour, oats, baking powder and salt in medium bowl. Add oil and just enough milk, 1 tablespoon at a time, until mixture forms a ball.

4. On lightly floured surface, roll dough into 12×9-inch rectangle. Place dough on prepared cookie sheet. Spread fig mixture in 2½-inch-wide strip lengthwise down center of rectangle. Make cuts almost to filling at ½-inch intervals on both 12-inch sides. Fold strips over filling, overlapping and crossing in center. Bake 15 to 18 minutes or until lightly browned.

5. To prepare icing, combine cream cheese, powdered sugar and vanilla in small bowl; mix well. Drizzle over bars.

Makes 12 servings

nutrients per serving:

Calories 104
Calories from Fat 26%
Protein 2g
Carbohydrate 18g

Fiber 1g
Total Fat 3g
Saturated Fat 1g
Cholesterol 1mg
Sodium 93mg

Fish

Fish is a smart catch for a healthy diet. The mild, delicately sweet flavor and quick cooking times make most varieties an excellent choice for weeknight meals.

benefits

Health experts recommend eating fish at least twice a week. It provides quality protein on par with meat but generally contains less total and saturated fat than even the leanest cuts of beef or chicken. What's more, the fat in fish is mostly unsaturated omega-3 oil, which has been linked to an amazing array of health benefits, from preventing heart disease and cancer, to treating arthritis, reducing inflammation, easing depression and improving memory. Excellent sources of omega-3 fats include salmon, mackerel, sardines, anchovies, trout, tuna, whitefish, bass, ocean perch and halibut.

selection and storage

Whether whole, fillets or steaks, fish should be firm and moist and not smell fishy. If you don't cook fresh fish the day you buy it, store it in the refrigerator for one day or wrap well and freeze. Fish will keep in the freezer up to six months.

preparation and serving tips

For leaner fish (most lighter color flesh), use moist-heat methods such as poaching, steaming or baking with vegetables. Dry-heat methods, such as baking, broiling and grilling, work well for fattier fish, like salmon and swordfish. Fish cooks fast; it's done when it looks opaque and the flesh just begins to flake. The rule of thumb is to bake for 8 to 10 minutes per inch of thickness, measured at the thickest point. For grilling or broiling, cook 4 to 5 minutes per inch of thickness.

nutrients per serving:

**Whitefish
3 ounces cooked**

Calories 146
Protein 21g
Total Fat 6g
Saturated Fat 1g
Cholesterol 65mg
Carbohydrate 0g
Dietary Fiber 0g
Sodium 55mg
Potassium 345mg
Phosphorus 294mg
Iron 0.4mg
Vitamin B₁₂ 0.8mcg
Selenium 14mcg

tilapia with spinach and feta

- 1 teaspoon olive oil
- 1 clove garlic, minced
- 4 cups baby spinach
- 2 skinless tilapia fillets (4 ounces each)
- ¼ teaspoon black pepper
- 2 ounces reduced-fat feta cheese,
    cut into 2 pieces

1. Preheat oven to 350°F. Spray baking sheet with nonstick cooking spray.

2. Heat oil in medium skillet over medium-low heat. Add garlic; cook and stir 1 minute. Add spinach; cook just until wilted, stirring occasionally.

3. Arrange fillets on prepared baking sheet; sprinkle with pepper. Place one piece of cheese on each fillet; top with spinach mixture.

4. Fold one end of each fillet up and over cheese and spinach filling; secure with toothpick. Repeat with opposite end of each fillet.

5. Bake about 20 minutes or until fish is firm and begins to flake when tested with fork.

Makes 2 servings

nutrients per serving:

Calories 193
Calories from Fat 41%
Protein 26g
Carbohydrate 3g
Fiber <1g
Total Fat 9g
Saturated Fat 3g
Cholesterol 10mg
Sodium 531mg

Flax Seed

Flax seed may be tiny, but it's mighty when it comes to health payoffs. To unlock its potential benefits, flax seed must be ground before eating.

benefits

Flax seed is best known for providing a healthy dose of alpha linolenic acid, the plant version of omega-3 fat. This form of unsaturated fat helps to fight inflammation that can lead to heart disease, cancer, diabetes and arthritis. This tiny seed is packed with soluble fiber, the kind that helps lower blood cholesterol levels. Flax seed is also rich in antioxidants and phytonutrients that may play a role in warding off breast cancer and protecting the intestines in those with inflammatory bowel disease.

selection and storage

Flax seed is available whole or already ground into meal. Because ground flax will go rancid more quickly, it's better to buy whole flax seed and grind it yourself (this takes seconds in a food processor or blender). Once ground, flax seed should be stored in an airtight container in the freezer and used within a few weeks. Whole flax seed stays fresh for up to a year if stored in a cool, dark, dry place.

preparation and serving tips

Flax seed has a pleasant nutty flavor, but it's almost undetectable when added to many foods. A few tablespoons of ground flax seed can be added to baked goods, such as breads, muffins, cookies and pancakes. Sprinkle it over cottage cheese, yogurt, cereal and salads or add it to smoothies. It can be added to meat loaves, meatballs and casseroles. Ground flax seed blended with water can also be used as an egg substitute in baked goods for people who can't, or choose not to, eat eggs.

nutrients per serving:

Flax Seed, ground
1 tablespoon

Calories 37
Protein 1g
Total Fat 3g
Saturated Fat 0g
Cholesterol 0mg
Carbohydrate 2g
Dietary Fiber 2g
Sodium 0mg
Potassium 60mg
Calcium 18mg
Iron 0.4mg
Phosphorus 45mg
Magnesium 27mg

Garlic

Over the centuries garlic has been credited with everything from increasing strength to curing toothaches to scaring away vampires. Garlic's unique flavor can be subtle and sweet or strong and piquant depending on how it is used.

benefits

Research suggests garlic can help lower high blood pressure and slow the hardening of arteries that can lead to heart attacks and strokes. Eating garlic also seems to lower the risk of stomach, colon and rectal cancers. And it may be effective at killing bacteria and reducing colds. (Garlic also thins the blood, so if you eat a lot of it, alert your doctor before any planned surgery.) Many of these benefits appear linked to allicin, the compound responsible for garlic's distinctive aroma and flavor, which is formed when garlic is crushed, finely chopped or cooked.

selection and storage

Pink-skinned (Italian) garlic is sweeter and milder than white (American) garlic. Elephant garlic, which is related to the leek, is the mildest of all. Choose garlic bulbs that are firm to the touch with no visible damp or brown spots. If you see a green sprout in the center of a garlic clove, remove it since it can taste bitter. Jarred garlic and garlic powder are convenient but lack the flavor of fresh.

preparation and serving tips

Use pressed or minced garlic when you want more garlic flavor to come through. For just a touch of garlic flavor, add a peeled, crushed whole clove to any dish and remove it before serving. To experience the suave, buttery side of garlic, roast an entire head until tender, then squeeze out the cloves. Cooked this way, garlic's flavor is mild enough to spread on bread.

nutrients per serving:

**Garlic
1 clove**

Calories 4
Protein 0g
Total Fat 0g
Saturated Fat 0g
Cholesterol 0mg
Carbohydrate 1g
Dietary Fiber 0g
Sodium 0mg
Potassium 10mg
Calcium 5mg
Iron 0.1mg
Vitamin C 1mg

Ginger

Aromatic and spicy, fresh ginger is an important spice in Asian and Indian cuisine. It has a long tradition in folk medicine of being good for the digestion with benefits that hold true today.

benefits

Ginger has traditionally been used as a remedy for gastrointestinal upset, and research supports its use for alleviating the symptoms of motion sickness, morning sickness related to pregnancy and even nausea associated with chemotherapy. Ginger is also rich in antioxidant substances that have anti-inflammatory effects, which may explain its apparent ability to reduce joint pain, swelling and stiffness in people with arthritis. Ginger's anti-inflammatory effects may also prove beneficial in combating cancer, heart disease and the growing list of other diseases linked to chronic inflammation in the body.

selection and storage

Fresh ginger is a knobby, bumpy-looking, beige-colored root available year-round in the produce section. Choose ginger that is fragrant and pale in color with an unwrinkled skin. Store fresh ginger at room temperature for up to three weeks, or for longer storage, freeze fresh ginger in a sealed bag and thaw slightly to slice off a portion for use. The powdered ginger used in baked goods comes from the same plant, but it has a different flavor and should not be substituted for fresh.

preparation and serving tips

Mature ginger has a thin, tough skin that must be peeled away. The tender though fibrous flesh can be minced, sliced or grated on a box grater. In stir-fries, minced ginger is usually added to the oil along with garlic to infuse flavor. For a lighter touch, whole ginger slices can be added while cooking and then removed before serving. Larger pieces of ginger remain tough and unpalatable even after cooking.

nutrients per serving:

**Ginger, fresh
1 tablespoon minced**

Calories 5
Protein 0g
Total Fat 0g
Saturated Fat 0g
Cholesterol 0mg
Carbohydrate 1g
Dietary Fiber 0g
Sodium 1mg
Potassium 25mg
Calcium 1mg
Magnesium 3mg

ginger noodles with sesame egg strips

5 egg whites

6 teaspoons teriyaki sauce, divided

3 teaspoons sesame seeds, toasted*
    divided

1 teaspoon dark sesame oil

½ cup fat-free reduced-sodium chicken
    broth

1 tablespoon minced fresh ginger

6 ounces Chinese rice noodles or
    vermicelli, cooked and well drained

⅓ cup sliced green onions

*To toast sesame seeds, spread in small skillet. Shake
skillet over medium heat 2 minutes or until seeds begin
to pop and turn golden.*

1. Beat egg whites, 2 teaspoons teriyaki sauce and 1 teaspoon sesame seeds in large bowl.

2. Heat oil in large nonstick skillet over medium heat. Pour egg mixture into skillet; cook 1½ to 2 minutes or until bottom is set. Turn over; cook 30 seconds to 1 minute. Slide onto plate; cool and cut into ½-inch strips.

3. Add broth, remaining 4 teaspoons teriyaki sauce and ginger to skillet. Bring to a boil over high heat; reduce heat to medium. Add noodles; heat through. Add egg strips and green onions; heat through. Sprinkle with remaining 2 teaspoons sesame seeds just before serving. *Makes 4 servings*

nutrients per serving:

Calories 111
Calories from Fat 19%
Protein 7g
Carbohydrate 16g
Fiber <1g

Total Fat 2g
Saturated Fat 1g
Cholesterol 0mg
Sodium 226mg

Grapefruit

The tangy, refreshing taste of grapefruit can really perk up your morning. A hybrid of orange and pomelo, this citrus offers a lot of nutrition for very few calories.

nutrients per serving:

Grapefruit
½ medium

Calories 41
Protein 1g
Total Fat 0g
Saturated Fat 0g
Cholesterol 0mg
Carbohydrate 10g
Dietary Fiber 1.5g
Sodium 0mg
Potassium 180mg
Calcium 15mg
Iron 0.1mg
Vitamin A 1,187 IU
Vitamin C 44mg
Folate 13mcg

benefits

Grapefruit is loaded with vitamin C, and the pink and red varieties are good sources of vitamin A in the form of beta-carotene. These vitamins, along with another antioxidant in grapefruit known as lycopene, help protect the body's cells from damage that can lead to cancer and other diseases. Grapefruit is also packed with powerful phytonutrients that help prevent certain age-related eye diseases. If you eat grapefruit's white membrane, you get a decent dose of cholesterol-lowering soluble fiber. Grapefruit and grapefruit juice can interfere with certain medications, however, so check your medication labels.

selection and storage

Although grapefruit is available year-round, peak season is from October through June. Whether white, pink or red, grapefruit's sweetness will vary depending on the variety, the growing season and shipping conditions. Choose grapefruit that have thin, brightly colored skin and feel heavy for their size. Avoid those that are soft and mushy. Store grapefruit in your refrigerator's crisper drawer, where they will keep for at least two weeks.

preparation and serving tips

Wash grapefruit before cutting it to prevent bacteria that might be on the skin from being introduced to the inside. For maximum flavor and juiciness, bring grapefruit to room temperature before eating. Beyond the typical halved grapefruit at breakfast, try peeling and eating it out of hand or add sections to salads. For dessert, sprinkle a grapefruit half with a little brown sugar and place it under the broiler until it bubbles.

cranberry fruit salad

- 2 large navel oranges
- 2 large pink grapefruit
- 1 cup seedless grapes
- 2 kiwi, peeled, halved lengthwise and sliced into bite-size pieces (½ cup)
- ¾ cup light cranberry juice cocktail
- 2 tablespoons dried cranberries

1. Grate orange peel to measure 1 teaspoon. Peel oranges and grapefruit. Cut fruit into segments over large bowl, leaving behind white pith. Squeeze pith and peels over bowl to extract any remaining juice.

2. Stir in grapes, kiwi, cranberry juice, cranberries and grated orange peel. Serve immediately.   *Makes 8 servings*

nutrients per serving:

Calories 70	**Fiber** 2g
Calories from Fat 0%	**Total Fat** 0g
Protein 1g	**Saturated Fat** 0g
Carbohydrate 18g	**Cholesterol** 0mg
	Sodium 0mg

Grapes

It's no wonder grapes were one of the very first fruits to be cultivated. Is there anything sweeter, more refreshing or more fun to eat than a bunch of grapes?

benefits

Grapes may not be packed with traditional nutrients, but they do contain an abundance of powerful health-preserving phytonutrients that researchers are just beginning to appreciate. Among them is resveratrol, an antioxidant found in the skin of red and purple grapes and in red wine. Resveratrol has shown promise in fighting cancer and in lowering the risk of heart disease and stroke by reducing potentially damaging blood clots, improving blood flow and interfering with the process by which cholesterol is deposited on artery walls.

nutrients per serving:

Grapes
½ cup

Calories 31
Protein 0g
Total Fat 0g
Saturated Fat 0g
Cholesterol 0mg
Carbohydrate 8g
Dietary Fiber <1g
Sodium 0mg
Potassium 90mg
Calcium 6mg
Iron 0.1mg
Vitamin A 46 IU
Vitamin C 2mg
Folate 2mcg

selection and storage

There are thousands of kinds of grapes (50 are grown in California alone) in a huge assortment of sizes and colors. Whatever the variety, look for clusters of plump fruit firmly attached to pliable, green stems. Whether green, red or blue/black, a deep even color is often the key to flavor. Grapes are very sensitive to moisture and may quickly develop mold or mildew, so store them without washing in the bag they came in. Refrigerated, they'll keep up to a week.

preparation and serving tips

Just before eating, thoroughly rinse grape clusters in a colander. Chilling enhances the flavor and texture of table grapes. Cold, sliced grapes taste great blended with low-fat yogurt. Frozen grapes make a popular summer treat. For a change of pace, skewer grapes with banana slices, apple chunks, pineapple cubes or any favorite fruit. Brush with a combination of honey, lemon juice and ground nutmeg. Broil until warm.

chocolate-drizzled frozen grapes

1 cup seedless grapes (green and red)
1 tablespoon semisweet chocolate chips
1 teaspoon fat-free (skim) milk
½ teaspoon powdered sugar
Fresh mint (optional)

1. Place grapes in single layer on baking sheet. Freeze 2 hours or up to 48 hours.

2. About 5 minutes before serving, place chocolate chips and milk in small microwavable cup. Microwave on HIGH 20 seconds; stir until chocolate is melted. If necessary, microwave additional 10 seconds or until chocolate is melted and smooth.

3. Remove grapes from freezer; divide evenly between two bowls. Sprinkle powdered sugar over grapes. Drizzle melted chocolate over grapes. Garnish with mint. Serve immediately.

Makes 2 servings

Note: To drizzle chocolate, place melted chocolate in resealable food storage bag. Snip off small piece from corner of bag and squeeze chocolate over grapes.

nutrients per serving:

Calories 81	**Total Fat** 2g
Calories from Fat 22%	**Saturated Fat** 1g
Protein 1g	**Cholesterol** 0mg
Carbohydrate 18g	**Sodium** 3mg
Fiber 1g	

Green Peas

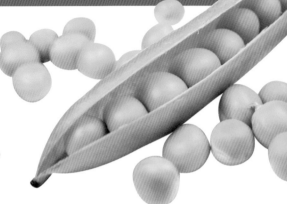

Freshly shelled peas are a springtime treat. Also known as English peas, they can be enjoyed raw or cooked. Like other legumes, peas are full of nutrients and low in calories.

benefits

Green peas supply twice the protein of most vegetables and a substantial amount of soluble fiber, making them ideal for reducing blood cholesterol and regulating blood sugar. Among the essential nutrients green peas provide are zinc, a primary ingredient of a strong immune system; iron, the mineral that carries oxygen throughout the body; and vitamin K and manganese, both important for healthy bones and proper blood clotting. Peas also supply lutein, a phytonutrient linked to decreased risk of macular degeneration, a common cause of blindness in older adults.

selection and storage

Fresh green peas are available during the spring and fall. Choose those that are firm, plump and in bright green pods. Because their sugar quickly turns to starch, the sooner you eat them the more flavorful they'll be. Store fresh peas in the refrigerator, but plan to eat them within a few days. Green peas are also convenient and nutritious in frozen and canned forms. Just be sure to rinse canned peas to lower the sodium.

preparation and serving tips

Wash fresh peas just before shelling. Steam fresh or frozen green peas a short time, 6 to 8 minutes, to retain flavor and vitamin C. Canned peas only need gentle heating to prevent them from getting mushy. Fresh raw peas make a great snack or addition to salads. Cooked peas add a welcome touch of color and texture to soups, casseroles and pasta dishes, and they are a must for a side of mixed vegetables.

nutrients per serving:

Green Peas ½ cup cooked		
Calories 67	**Saturated Fat** 0g	**Calcium** 22mg
Protein 4g	**Cholesterol** 0mg	**Iron** 1.2mg
Total Fat 0g	**Carbohydrate** 13g	**Vitamin A** 641 IU
	Dietary Fiber 4.5g	**Vitamin C** 11mg
	Sodium 0mg	**Folate** 50mcg
	Potassium 220mg	

nutrients per serving:

Calories 175
Calories from Fat 7%
Protein 19g

Carbohydrate 19g
Fiber 2g
Total Fat 1g
Saturated Fat <1g
Cholesterol 97mg
Sodium 152mg

shrimp and chicken paella

¾ cup cooked rice
2 cans (about 14 ounces each) no-salt-added diced tomatoes
½ teaspoon ground turmeric *or* ⅛ teaspoon saffron threads
1 package (¾ pound) medium raw shrimp, peeled and deveined (about 3 cups)
2 chicken tenders (about 4 ounces), cut into 1-inch pieces
1 cup frozen peas

1. Preheat oven to 400°F. Lightly coat 8-inch glass baking dish with nonstick cooking spray. Spread rice in dish.

2. Pour 1 can of tomatoes with juice over rice; sprinkle with turmeric. Arrange shrimp and chicken over tomatoes. Top with peas.

3. Drain remaining can of tomatoes; discard juice. Spread tomatoes evenly over shrimp and chicken. Cover; bake 30 minutes. Let stand, covered, 5 minutes before serving.

Makes 4 servings

Hazelnuts

Also known as filberts, these small, meaty nuts that look a bit like an acorn add unique flavor, texture and nutrition to sweet and savory foods.

benefits

Hazelnuts are an excellent source of several nutrients known to protect your heart, including fiber, B vitamins, vitamin E and arginine, an amino acid that relaxes blood vessels.

nutrients per serving:

**Hazelnuts, dry roasted
1 ounce**

Calories 183
Protein 4g
Total Fat 18g
Saturated Fat 1.5g
Cholesterol 0mg
Carbohydrate 5g
Dietary Fiber 3g
Sodium 0mg
Potassium 215mg
Calcium 35mg
Iron 1.3mg
Vitamin A 17 IU
Vitamin C 1mg
Folate 25mcg
Vitamin E 4mg
Magnesium 49mg

Among nuts, hazelnuts have one of the lowest saturated fat percentages (along with pine nuts and almonds) and are one of the best nut sources of heart-healthy unsaturated fats, which can help lower blood cholesterol and reduce the risk of cardiovascular disease, especially when they replace saturated fats in the diet. Because they are rich in protein, hazelnuts also make a satisfying snack. Still, be sure to moderate your intake; like all nuts, they are relatively high in calories.

selection and storage

Hazelnuts can be purchased in the shell or out and sometimes chopped or ground as well. You would need to shell about 1 pound of hazelnuts to yield 1½ cups of nutmeats. Once shelled, hazelnuts should be eaten as soon as possible. Store unopened packages up to four months in the refrigerator or twice as long in the freezer. Hazelnut oil and hazelnut flour are also available.

preparation and serving tips

The papery brown skin on shelled hazelnuts can be bitter. To remove it, spread hazelnuts on a baking sheet and roast at 300°F for 10 to 15 minutes or until the skins begin to peel. Roll the toasted nuts in a clean kitchen towel and let them rest 10 minutes. Rub the nuts in the towel and most of the skins will come off. Hazelnuts' flavor pairs particularly well with chocolate and coffee.

Jicama

Sometimes referred to as a Mexican potato, this easily overlooked root vegetable is refreshingly crisp and crunchy, with a mild, nutty flavor and radishlike texture.

benefits

Jicama is very low in calories and almost sodium free. It is also an excellent source of vitamin C, which helps fuel your immune system; promotes healthy bones, teeth and gums; and helps protect your blood vessels from damage that can lead to a heart attack or stroke. Because it contains ample fiber and a lot of water, jicama is helpful for appetite control. It fills you up for few calories and it takes a while to chew, allowing time for fullness signals to reach your brain before you overeat.

selection and storage

Jicama is in season from November through May and is available in Latin American markets and many large supermarkets. Select jicama that is firm and without bruises or wrinkles. Jicama can be stored for up to two weeks in a plastic bag in the refrigerator.

preparation and serving tips

Jicama adds great crunch and a fresh, mild flavor to foods. The thin, tan skin should be peeled before eating or cooking. Cut jicama into cubes or sticks and add it to salads, salsa or coleslaw, or simply enjoy it as a snack. It can also be added to stir-fries, where it can stand in for water chestnuts, or roasted with other vegetables. Even cooked, jicama stays firm. For a refreshing salad, combine raw cubed jicama, sliced cucumber and orange sections; sprinkle with chili powder and salt and drizzle with lemon juice.

nutrients per serving:

Jicama
½ cup raw

Calories 25
Protein <1g
Total Fat 0g
Saturated Fat 0g
Cholesterol 0mg
Carbohydrate 6g
Dietary Fiber 3g
Sodium 5mg
Potassium 100mg
Calcium 8mg
Iron 0.4mg
Vitamin A 14 IU
Vitamin C 13mg
Folate 8mcg

Kale

Kale comes in a gorgeous bouquet of dark green, frilly leaves often tinged with magenta. It's a member of the nutritious cabbage family, but with a milder flavor and softer texture.

nutrients per serving:

Kale
½ cup cooked

Calories 18
Protein 1g
Total Fat 0g
Saturated Fat 0g
Cholesterol 0mg
Carbohydrate 4g
Dietary Fiber 1.5g
Sodium 15mg
Potassium 150mg
Calcium 47mg
Iron 0.6mg
Vitamin A 8,854 IU
Vitamin C 26mg
Folate 8mcg

benefits

Kale stands a head above other greens as an excellent source of beta-carotene and vitamin C, two antioxidants believed to be major players in the body's battle against cancer, heart disease and certain age-related chronic diseases. Kale is also a phenomenal source of readily absorbed calcium, a mineral that is vital to warding off osteoporosis, may reduce symptoms of premenstrual syndrome and may help keep blood pressure in a healthy range. Kale also provides decent amounts of folate, iron and potassium.

selection and storage

There are several varieties of kale, the most common being curly kale, which has ruffled leaves and a fibrous stalk. Tuscan, or dinosaur, kale has flat, blue-green leaves with a bumpy surface. Prime season is midwinter through spring. Choose small, deeply colored leaves with no wilting or yellowing. For the sweetest, mildest flavor, store kale in the refrigerator crisper for no more than five days before using it.

preparation and serving tips

Wash kale thoroughly before cooking, as it often has dirt and sand in its leaves, and remove any tough center stems. Keep cooking time to a minimum to preserve nutrients. Steaming chopped kale for 5 minutes is usually enough. Like most greens, kale cooks down a great deal; 1 pound of raw yields about ½ cup of cooked. Kale works well with pasta and in soups and stews.

Kiwi

The brown, fuzzy outside of kiwi hides a gorgeous emerald green interior loaded with nutrition. Kiwi's sweet-tart taste and distinctive color can jazz up salads, desserts and even drinks.

benefits

One medium kiwi provides an entire day's worth of vitamin C, which not only helps maintain teeth and gums but may protect arteries, including those feeding the heart and brain, from damage. Kiwi also packs potassium for healthy blood pressure and the antioxidants lutein and zeaxanthin that safeguard the eyes. The fruit's flesh contains soluble fiber, which helps reduce blood cholesterol, and its little black seeds contribute insoluble fiber, which promotes regularity.

selection and storage

Kiwis are available year-round. Choose those that are fragrant and fairly firm but give under gentle pressure. Firm kiwis need about a week to ripen at room temperature; speed ripening by placing them in a closed paper bag for one to two days. Ripe kiwis keep for one to two weeks in the refrigerator.

preparation and serving tips

With their brilliant green color and inner circle of tiny black seeds, sliced kiwis shine in fruit and vegetable salads. They don't even discolor when exposed to air since they contain so much antioxidant vitamin C.

Most people prefer eating peeled kiwi, though the skin is edible. Just wash them and rub off the brown fuzz. For a handheld treat, cut an unpeeled kiwi in half and scoop out the flesh with a spoon. Since kiwi contains an enzyme that prevents gelatin from setting, you'll want to leave it out of molded salads.

nutrients per serving:

Kiwi
1 medium

Calories 42
Protein 1g
Total Fat 0g
Saturated Fat 0g
Cholesterol 0mg
Carbohydrate 10g
Dietary Fiber 2g
Sodium 0mg
Potassium 215mg
Calcium 23mg
Iron 0.2mg
Vitamin A 60 IU
Vitamin C 64mg
Folate 17mcg

95

Lemons

Sunshiny lemons are appreciated in cuisines around the world for adding zest to both the savory and the sweet. Their tartness can make you pucker, but without lemon many foods would indeed be dull.

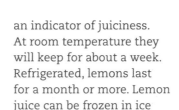

benefits

Lemons are loaded with vitamin C, a nutrient the body needs to heal wounds and perform all sorts of daily maintenance. For example, vitamin C is important for making collagen, a protein the body uses to grow and repair blood vessels, skin, cartilage, ligaments, tendons, bones and teeth. Vitamin C is also an antioxidant that helps fight off heart disease, inflammation and cancer. The lemon's outer peel, or zest, is rich in yet another antioxidant called rutin, which may further help protect against heart disease by helping to strengthen blood vessel walls.

selection and storage

Look for unblemished, thin-skinned lemons that are heavy for their size— an indicator of juiciness. At room temperature they will keep for about a week. Refrigerated, lemons last for a month or more. Lemon juice can be frozen in ice cube trays for later use.

preparation and serving tips

To get more juice from a lemon, bring it to room temperature, then roll it back and forth on a countertop before you cut and squeeze it. If a recipe calls for lemon peel or zest, wash the lemon thoroughly and remove the outermost yellow layer with a grater, zester or vegetable peeler. Avoid the white pith, which is bitter tasting. A squeeze of lemon can often take the place of salt, and a slice of lemon in a glass of water not only looks pretty, it makes for a refreshing beverage.

nutrients per serving:

**Lemon
Juice of 1 medium**

Calories 12
Protein <1g
Total Fat 0g
Saturated Fat 0g
Cholesterol 0mg
Carbohydrate 4g
Dietary Fiber 0.2g
Sodium 0mg
Potassium 58mg
Calcium 3mg
Vitamin A 9 IU
Vitamin C 22mg
Folate 6mcg

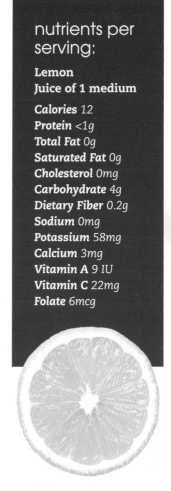

lemony greek kabobs

1 pound beef top sirloin steak
  (1 inch thick), cut into 16 pieces
¼ cup fat-free Italian salad dressing
3 tablespoons fresh lemon juice, divided
1 tablespoon dried oregano
1 tablespoon Worcestershire sauce
2 teaspoons dried basil
1 teaspoon grated lemon peel
⅛ teaspoon red pepper flakes
1 large green bell pepper, cut into
  16 pieces
16 cherry tomatoes
2 teaspoons olive oil
⅛ teaspoon salt

1. Combine beef, salad dressing, 2 tablespoons lemon juice, oregano, Worcestershire sauce, basil, lemon peel and red pepper flakes in large resealable food storage bag. Seal bag; turn to coat. Marinate in refrigerator at least 8 hours or overnight, turning occasionally.

2. Preheat broiler. Thread four 10-inch skewers with beef, alternating with bell pepper and tomatoes. Spray rimmed baking sheet or broiler pan with nonstick cooking spray. Brush kabobs with marinade; place on prepared baking sheet. Discard remaining marinade. Broil kabobs 3 minutes. Turn over; broil 2 minutes or until desired doneness. Remove to serving platter.

3. Add remaining 1 tablespoon lemon juice, oil and salt to pan drippings on baking sheet; stir well, scraping up brown bits from bottom of pan. Drizzle juices over kabobs.

Makes 4 servings

nutrients per serving:

Calories 193
Calories from Fat 37%

Protein 25g
Carbohydrate 5g
Fiber 1g
Total Fat 8g
Saturated Fat 2g
Cholesterol 69mg
Sodium 159mg

Lentils

Like other legumes, lentils are versatile as well as nutritious. Their mild, earthy flavor works well with many spices and flavor profiles. Lentils complement the dish without overwhelming it.

benefits

Lentils carry a rich load of soluble fiber to help lower blood cholesterol and steady blood sugar.

nutrients per serving:

Lentils
½ cup cooked

Calories 115
Protein 9g
Total Fat 0g
Saturated Fat 0g
Cholesterol 0mg
Carbohydrate 20g
Dietary Fiber 8g
Sodium 0mg
Potassium 365mg
Calcium 19mg
Iron 3.3mg
Vitamin A 8 IU
Vitamin C 2mg
Folate 179mcg

For people who don't eat much (or any) red meat, lentils make an excellent substitute as a source of iron, the mineral essential for carrying oxygen to the body's cells. Lentils are also exceptionally high in folate, a vitamin that is especially valuable to pregnant women because it helps prevent certain birth defects. Research suggests folate may also help fight off heart disease and dementia.

selection and storage

Lentils come in various shades of red, green and black, but the most common variety is brown. If buying them packaged, look for well-sealed bags without signs of moisture. The disc-shaped lentils inside should be brightly colored and uncracked. If you buy in bulk, ensure the lentils are fresh and free from insect infestation. When stored in a well-sealed container at a cool temperature, lentils keep for up to a year.

preparation and serving tips

Lentils do not need to be soaked and most cook in about 30 minutes. Before cooking, sort through dry lentils and remove any dirt or foreign particles. For salads or sides where you want lentils to keep their shape, use brown lentils and don't overcook them. For purées, dips or creamy soups, try red lentils, which become velvety soft in about 15 minutes.

lentils, pepper & feta rice

½ cup sun-dried tomatoes, packed in oil
2 cups chopped green bell peppers
1 cup chopped onion
6 cups water
8 ounces dried brown lentils, rinsed and sorted
1 tablespoon Italian seasoning
½ teaspoon salt
6 ounces extra-lean ham, finely chopped
2 cups uncooked instant brown rice
4 ounces crumbled feta cheese

1. Drain tomatoes, reserving 1 teaspoon oil. Rinse tomatoes under hot water; drain well and pat dry. Chop tomatoes.

2. Add reserved oil to Dutch oven; heat over medium heat. Add bell peppers, onion and tomatoes; cook and stir 4 minutes or until tender.

3. Add water; bring to a boil. Add lentils, Italian seasoning and salt. Reduce heat; cover and simmer 30 minutes or until lentils are tender. Remove from heat; stir in ham. Cover and let stand 10 minutes.

4. Meanwhile, cook rice according to package directions.

5. Serve rice with lentil mixture; sprinkle with feta cheese. _Makes 8 servings_

nutrients per serving:

Calories 350
Calories from Fat 15%
Protein 18g
Carbohydrate 57g
Fiber 6g
Total Fat 6g
Saturated Fat 3g
Cholesterol 25mg
Sodium 550mg

Lettuce

Lettuce can be crunchy or feather light. It can come in loose leaves or a compact head and a rainbow of different colors. Shredded, in a salad or on a sandwich, it's almost calorie free!

nutrients per serving:

**Lettuce, romaine
1 cup**

Calories 8
Protein 1g
Total Fat 0g
Saturated Fat 0g
Cholesterol 0mg
Carbohydrate 2g
Dietary Fiber 1g
Sodium 5mg
Potassium 115mg
Calcium 16mg
Iron 0.5mg
Vitamin A 4,094 IU
Vitamin C 11mg
Folate 64mcg

benefits

The rule of thumb for choosing nutrient-packed lettuce is to look for varieties with dark green or other deeply colored leaves. For example, deep green romaine has five times the vitamin C of pale iceberg lettuce and contains more beta-carotene, calcium, potassium and folate, too. Other nutrient-rich varieties include endive, escarole, looseleaf, butterhead, arugula and watercress. They're all very low in calories and fat free and provide tummy-filling fiber, which is why a salad is a great meal starter if you're watching your blood cholesterol, blood pressure or weight.

selection and storage

There are hundreds of varieties of lettuce, offering plenty of choices in the supermarket. Bagged lettuce labeled "mesclun" isn't a variety, it's a mix of different small lettuces and herbs. Lettuce should be refrigerated, unwashed, in the original bag where it will keep for about a week. Prewashed salad greens are a convenient option, but once opened they can become slimy and unusable in three or four days.

preparation and serving tips

For heads of lettuce, remove the core and separate the leaves. Wash, drain completely and dry in a salad spinner or blot with paper towels. Lettuce can be combined with fresh fruits or vegetables, cold pasta or chunks of chicken or tuna to make low-calorie, highly nutritious main dishes. Just go easy on the salad dressing and high-calorie toppings. For a homemade salad dressing, combine flavored vinegar or lemon juice with olive oil and some herbs in a covered jar. Shake to combine and pour on right before serving.

layered mexican salad

- 1 package (10 ounces) shredded lettuce
- ½ cup chopped green onions
- ½ cup fat-free sour cream
- ⅓ cup medium picante sauce
- 1 medium lime, halved
- 1 teaspoon sugar
- ½ teaspoon ground cumin
- 1 medium avocado, chopped
- ¾ cup (3 ounces) shredded reduced-fat sharp Cheddar cheese
- 2 ounces baked tortilla chips, coarsely crumbled

1. Arrange lettuce evenly in 13×9-inch dish. Sprinkle with green onions.

2. Stir together sour cream, picante sauce, juice from half of lime, sugar and cumin in small bowl. Spoon evenly over lettuce and green onions. Place avocado evenly over sour cream layer. Squeeze remaining lime half evenly over avocado layer. Sprinkle evenly with cheese.

3. Cover with plastic wrap. Refrigerate until serving. Sprinkle with crumbled tortilla chips before serving. *Makes 8 servings*

Variation: Add chopped fresh tomatoes to avocado layer. Sprinkle chopped fresh cilantro over chips.

nutrients per serving:

Calories 118	**Fiber** 3g
Calories from Fat 38%	**Total Fat** 5g
Protein 5g	**Saturated Fat** 2g
Carbohydrate 13g	**Cholesterol** 10mg
	Sodium 208mg

Limes

With their flowery aroma and refreshing acidic flavor, limes brighten everything from margaritas to ceviche to key lime pie. The fact that they're high in vitamin C is just another reason to make them your favorite squeeze.

benefits

Limes are loaded with vitamin C, and diets filled with C-rich foods have been linked to lower rates of high blood pressure, heart disease and cancer. Limes and other citrus fruits also pack an antioxidant phytochemical called limonin, which has shown anticancer, anti-inflammatory, antiviral and cholesterol-lowering effects in laboratory tests. Limes can even make it easier to trim fat from your diet. By taking advantage of limes' meat-tenderizing ability, you can enjoy leaner cuts of meat—the kind recommended in guidelines for lowering blood cholesterol and blood pressure.

selection and storage

The most common variety is the Persian lime. The key lime—of pie fame—is small and round, while the Persian looks more like a green lemon. Key limes are generally more flavorful because of their greater acidity. You'll find them readily available and affordable at Latin American markets. Limes will keep in the refrigerator for several weeks. For longer storage, freeze the juice in ice cube trays. Once frozen, pop out the cubes and transfer to a freezer bag until you need them.

preparation and serving tips

Lime juice makes a tenderizing addition to marinades for meat and poultry. Be careful to leave it on for only a short time, however, or the meat will become mushy. Lime zest adds a potent dose of flavor to salads, dressings and desserts. A squeeze of lime goes well with avocado, melon or papaya, and a lime wedge makes a natural accompaniment to seafood, chicken or Mexican dishes.

nutrients per serving:

Lime
Juice of 1 medium

Calories 11
Protein 0g
Total Fat 0g
Saturated Fat 0g
Cholesterol 0mg
Carbohydrate 4g
Dietary Fiber 0g
Sodium 1mg
Potassium 51.5mg
Calcium 6.2mg
Vitamin A 22 IU
Vitamin C 13.2mg
Folate 4.4mcg

roasted chili turkey breast with cilantro-lime rice

Turkey

- 1½ tablespoons chili powder
- 2 teaspoons dried oregano
- 1½ teaspoons ground cumin
- ½ teaspoon red pepper flakes
- ½ teaspoon salt
- ½ teaspoon black pepper
- 1 bone-in turkey breast with skin
  (5 pounds)

Rice

- 2 medium red bell peppers, chopped
- 2½ cups water
- 1½ cups quick-cooking brown rice
- ½ teaspoon ground turmeric
- 1 cup chopped green onions
- ½ cup chopped fresh cilantro
- 3 tablespoons olive oil
- 1 tablespoon grated lime peel
- 2 to 3 tablespoons lime juice
- ¾ teaspoon salt

1. Preheat oven to 325°F. Spray roasting pan and rack with nonstick cooking spray. Combine chili powder, oregano, cumin, pepper flakes, salt and black pepper in small bowl.

2. Separate turkey skin from meat by sliding fingers under skin. Spread chili mixture evenly over meat. Place turkey breast on prepared rack in roasting pan, skin side up.

3. Roast 1 hour and 30 minutes or until temperature reaches 165°F. Cover loosely with foil; let stand 10 to 15 minutes. Remove and discard skin, if desired.

4. Meanwhile, combine bell peppers, water, rice and turmeric in large saucepan. Bring to a boil. Reduce heat; cover and simmer 10 minutes or until liquid evaporates. Stir in green onions, cilantro, oil, lime peel, lime juice and salt. Serve rice with turkey.

Makes 12 servings

nutrients per serving:

Calories 218
Calories from Fat 29%
Protein 26g
Carbohydrate 12g
Fiber 2g
Total Fat 7g
Saturated Fat 1g
Cholesterol 77mg
Sodium 303mg

Mango

No wonder the mango is sometimes called the king of fruits. It is beautiful, fragrant and offers a wealth of nutrients along with a unique taste of tropical sweetness.

benefits

Mangoes are a superior source of beta-carotene, a vitamin A precursor and antioxidant linked to a reduced risk of some forms of cancer. And just one mango provides almost an entire day's worth of vitamin C, a powerful antioxidant and important player in infection control. Mangoes also contribute calcium, potassium and magnesium, and regularly consuming foods rich in these three minerals is associated with lower blood pressure.

selection and storage

There are more than 200 varieties of mangoes with colors ranging from yellow to bright red and orange. Choose those that feel firm but yield to slight pressure. The color should have begun to change from green to yellow, orange or red. You can speed the process by placing a mango in a paper bag for a few days. Mango is also available canned or frozen.

preparation and serving tips

The tricky part of preparing a mango is cutting the flesh away from the long, flat pit in the center. The thicker part of mango flesh is on the flatter sides of the mango. Stand the mango on end and slice the fruit from stem to tip, coming as close as you can to the pit. Lay each mango half skin side down and score the flesh in a crosshatch pattern without cutting through the skin. Then turn the piece inside out. The cubes of mango will be easy to slice away provided you can resist nibbling them then and there.

nutrients per serving:

Mango ½ medium		
Calories 101	Saturated Fat 0g	Magnesium 17mg
Protein 1g	Cholesterol 0mg	Calcium 18mg
Total Fat 0.5g	Carbohydrate 25g	Vitamin A 1,818 IU
	Dietary Fiber 2.5g	Vitamin C 61mg
	Sodium 0mg	Folate 72mcg
	Potassium 280mg	

spanish-style pork with mango salsa

2 teaspoons canola oil
¾ cup coarsely chopped onion
2 cloves garlic, minced
¾ pound pork tenderloin, cut into 1-inch cubes
1 teaspoon ground cinnamon
1 teaspoon ground cumin
1 teaspoon dried oregano
½ teaspoon ground coriander
¼ teaspoon salt
1½ cups chopped mango
1 cup chunky salsa
2 cups cooked brown rice
2 tablespoons slivered almonds, toasted (optional)

1. Heat oil in large nonstick skillet over medium-high heat. Add onion; cook and stir 4 minutes or until tender. Add garlic; cook and stir 30 seconds. Add pork, cinnamon, cumin, oregano, coriander and salt; cook and stir 5 to 6 minutes or until pork is well browned on all sides.

2. Reduce heat to medium-low. Stir in mango and salsa. Cover and cook 3 to 4 minutes or until heated through. Serve over rice. Sprinkle with almonds, if desired.   *Makes 4 servings*

Milk

Cow's milk has been a part of the human diet for thousands of years. Today we enjoy milk's amazing nutrition in dozens of ways. We pour it over our cereal, use it in our baked goods and drink it by the glass.

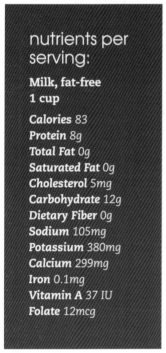

nutrients per serving:

Milk, fat-free
1 cup

Calories 83
Protein 8g
Total Fat 0g
Saturated Fat 0g
Cholesterol 5mg
Carbohydrate 12g
Dietary Fiber 0g
Sodium 105mg
Potassium 380mg
Calcium 299mg
Iron 0.1mg
Vitamin A 37 IU
Folate 12mcg

benefits

Milk contains high levels of good-quality protein and nine essential nutrients, but it's best known for its calcium, phosphorus and vitamin D, which are necessary for building bone and helping to prevent osteoporosis. Drinking low-fat or fat-free milk has also been linked to lower blood pressure. Some research suggests that people who drink milk and get more calcium and vitamin D in their diets are less likely to develop colon cancer. And some studies in animals and humans indicate consuming low-fat milk and other low-fat dairy products can aid weight control.

selection and storage

Milk varies in the percentage of fat, from whole (4%) to reduced-fat (2%), low-fat (1%) and fat-free, or skim. There are significant fat and calorie savings between whole and fat-free milk, but no difference in vitamin and mineral content. All milk containers have a "sell-by" date; the milk inside will stay fresh for about seven days after this date. Avoid raw (unpasteurized) milk, as it may carry bacteria that can make you sick. Powdered milk is also available.

preparation and serving tips

Milk tastes best when it's served icy cold. Most recipes that call for milk work fine with lower-fat varieties—an easy way to cut calories and fat. Try using a can of evaporated milk when you need milk with extra "body," such as in a cream soup or to add to coffee. Powdered milk makes a great addition to blender drinks, soups and casseroles, providing a low-calorie boost of calcium and protein to your favorite dishes.

rice pudding with dried cherries and berries

- 1½ cups water
- ¾ cup quick-cooking brown rice
- ½ cup dried cherries or cranberries
- 1¾ cups fat-free (skim) milk
- 1 package (4-serving size) vanilla fat-free sugar-free instant pudding and pie filling mix
- ½ teaspoon ground cinnamon
- ⅛ teaspoon salt
- 1 cup fresh or frozen blueberries, thawed
- 1 tablespoon powdered sugar
- ¼ teaspoon vanilla

1. Combine water, rice and cherries in medium saucepan; bring to a boil. Reduce heat; cover and simmer 12 minutes or until water is absorbed and rice is tender.

2. Whisk milk, pudding mix, cinnamon and salt in medium bowl 2 minutes or until thickened. Combine blueberries, sugar and vanilla in small bowl; toss gently to coat.

3. Add cooked rice to pudding mixture; stir well. Serve topped with blueberry mixture.

Makes 8 servings

nutrients per serving:

Calories 142
Calories from Fat 3%
Protein 3g
Carbohydrate 32g
Fiber 2g
Total Fat 1g
Saturated Fat 1g
Cholesterol 1mg
Sodium 218mg

Mushrooms

Few good-for-you foods offer the rich, satisfying flavor of mushrooms. They bring a subtle, earthy taste to almost any dish.

benefits

Mushrooms are low in calories and fat and are sodium and cholesterol free, plus they provide important nutrients, including B vitamins, vitamin D, selenium and potassium. Mushrooms are the only source of vitamin D in the produce aisle, naturally producing the vitamin following exposure to sunlight (just as humans do). Vitamin D is essential for bone health and is also being studied for its role in preventing cancer, heart disease and diabetes. Many varieties of mushrooms are also rich in phytonutrients that, together with the antioxidant mineral selenium, exhibit cancer-fighting properties.

selection and storage

All supermarkets stock white button mushrooms, and most also offer brown cremini, which are a slightly different strain of the white with a firmer texture and richer flavor. Portobello mushrooms are creminis that have been allowed to grow large. Look for plump, unwrinkled mushrooms without signs of moisture or shriveling. Prepackaged mushrooms can stay in their original container in the refrigerator. Loose mushrooms should be stored in a paper bag or ventilated container, but not in the crisper drawer.

Mushrooms only keep peak freshness and flavor for a few days.

preparation and serving tips

To clean mushrooms, wipe with a damp cloth or rinse briefly and dry thoroughly. Never soak mushrooms or they become soggy. Portobello mushrooms have dark gills under their caps, which are perfectly edible but sometimes scraped away so that they don't darken other ingredients. Mushrooms can be added to many vegetarian dishes to add a depth of flavor that can take the place of meat.

nutrients per serving:

**Mushrooms
½ cup cooked**

Calories 22
Protein 2g
Total Fat 1g
Saturated Fat 0g

Cholesterol 0mg
Carbohydrate 4g
Dietary Fiber 2g
Sodium 0mg
Potassium 278mg
Calcium 5mg

Iron 1.4mg
Vitamin D 16.4 IU
Selenium 9mcg
Niacin 3.5mg
Riboflavin 0.2mg

grilled portobello sandwiches

2 tablespoons extra virgin olive oil
1½ tablespoons balsamic vinegar
1 tablespoon coarse grain Dijon mustard
1 tablespoon water
1 teaspoon dried oregano
1 clove garlic, minced
½ teaspoon black pepper
¼ teaspoon salt
4 large portobello mushroom caps
    Nonstick cooking spray
8 slices multigrain Italian bread (8 ounces)
¼ cup (1 ounce) crumbled reduced-fat
    blue cheese
2 to 3 ounces spring greens

1. Combine oil, vinegar, mustard, water, oregano, garlic, pepper and salt in medium bowl. Place mushrooms on sheet of foil or large plate. Brush 2 tablespoons dressing over mushrooms; set aside remaining dressing. Let mushrooms stand 30 minutes.

2. Spray grill pan with cooking spray; heat over medium-high heat. Spray both sides of bread slices with cooking spray. Grill bread 1 minute on each side, pressing down with spatula to flatten slightly. Set aside.

3. Grill mushrooms 3 to 4 minutes per side or until tender. Place each mushroom on one bread slice. Sprinkle with blue cheese.

4. Combine spring greens and reserved dressing. Arrange spring greens on top of mushrooms; top with remaining bread slices.

Makes 4 sandwiches

nutrients per serving:

Calories 275
Calories from Fat 33%
Protein 9g
Carbohydrate 36g
Fiber 3g
Total Fat 10g
Saturated Fat 2g
Cholesterol 4mg
Sodium 590mg

Nectarines

A nectarine is a fuzzless variety of peach, and like a peach it can be white or yellow, freestone or clingstone. The luscious sweet juiciness of a nectarine almost tastes like a perfect summer day.

benefits

Nectarines are especially high in beta-carotene, a powerful cell-protecting antioxidant that the body converts to vitamin A. Their flesh is rich in phytonutrients that help protect against cancer, and it provides soluble fiber that helps lower blood cholesterol levels. And their skin contributes insoluble fiber, which helps to prevent constipation. Nectarines are also a good source of potassium, a mineral that's essential for controlling blood pressure.

selection and storage

Nectarines are in season from midspring to late September and at their very best in July and August. Choose nectarines that are firm yet give slightly to the touch. The reddish blush of a nectarine doesn't indicate ripeness. Instead, look for a uniform yellow background color with no green around the stem end. Avoid fruit with bruises or blemishes as well as those that are rock hard. Slightly underripe nectarines will ripen and soften at room temperature within a couple of days. Refrigerate to help slow ripening, but use within five days. Nectarines and peaches can be used interchangeably.

preparation and serving tips

A perfectly ripe nectarine needs no accompaniment other than a napkin or two to catch excess juice. Sliced nectarines make a delicious topping for yogurt or cottage cheese and can be used in a variety of fresh or cooked desserts. The flesh will darken when exposed to air, so sprinkle with lemon juice to prevent browning in fresh salads or uncooked desserts.

nutrients per serving:

Nectarine
1 medium

Calories 62
Protein 2g
Total Fat 0g
Saturated Fat 0g
Cholesterol 0mg
Carbohydrate 15g
Dietary Fiber 2.5g
Sodium 0mg
Potassium 285mg
Calcium 9mg
Vitamin A 471 IU
Vitamin C 8mg
Folate 7mcg

nectarine-raspberry cobbler

3 cups sliced peeled nectarines
(about 1¼ pounds)
½ cup raspberries
3 tablespoons sucralose-sugar blend,
divided
1 tablespoon cornstarch
½ teaspoon ground cinnamon
¾ cup all-purpose flour
1 teaspoon grated lemon peel
¾ teaspoon baking powder
¼ teaspoon salt
⅛ teaspoon baking soda
3 tablespoons cold margarine, cut into
pieces
½ cup reduced-fat buttermilk

1. Preheat oven to 375°F. Place nectarines and raspberries in large bowl. Combine 2 tablespoons sucralose-sugar blend, cornstarch and cinnamon in small bowl. Add to fruit; toss to coat. Place fruit mixture in 8-inch round baking dish.

2. Combine flour, lemon peel, baking powder, salt, baking soda and remaining 1 tablespoon sucralose-sugar blend in medium bowl. Cut in margarine with pastry blender or two knives until mixture resembles coarse crumbs. Stir in buttermilk until blended. Drop dough in six equal spoonfuls over fruit.

3. Bake 25 to 27 minutes or until biscuit topping begins to brown and fruit is bubbly. Serve warm. *Makes 6 servings*

nutrients per serving:

Calories 188
Calories from Fat 29%
Protein 3g
Carbohydrate 29g
Fiber 2g
Total Fat 6g
Saturated Fat 1g
Cholesterol 0mg
Sodium 283mg

Oats

Oats are a whole grain—whether instant, quick, old-fashioned or steel-cut—because they contain a fiber-rich bran layer along with other nutritious parts of the oat kernel.

nutrients per serving:

Oats
½ cup cooked

Calories 83
Protein 3g
Total Fat 2g
Saturated Fat 0g
Cholesterol 0mg
Carbohydrate 14g
Dietary Fiber 2g
Sodium 5mg
Potassium 80mg
Calcium 11mg
Iron 1.1mg
Thiamin 0.1mg
Niacin 0.3mg
Folate 7mcg

benefits

The fiber in oats can help decrease the risk of heart disease and diabetes. One way it defends your heart is by lowering blood levels of total and LDL ("bad") cholesterol. Indeed, research has shown that eating 3 grams of soluble fiber daily—the amount in 2 cups of oatmeal or 1 cup of cooked oat bran—can reduce blood cholesterol in three months. Oats' soluble fiber helps fend off diabetes, itself a risk factor for heart disease, by slowing sugar absorption and keeping the blood sugar level more even.

selection and storage

Cooking time and texture are the only differences among the varieties of oats. Chewy steel-cut oats are whole oats sliced into thick pieces; they take about 20 minutes to cook. Old-fashioned oats, or rolled oats, are steamed and flattened, so they take about 5 minutes to cook. Quick oats are cut into smaller pieces before being rolled, so they cook in about a minute. Instant oats are precooked, so it takes only boiling water to reconstitute them. Instant oats may have added sodium; flavored versions also have added sugar. Store oats in a dark, dry location in a well-sealed container for up to a year.

preparation and serving tips

Oats are commonly used as breakfast cereal or to make cookies, but they can also be added to dishes to boost fiber and nutrition, including meat loaves, burgers and fish cakes. Oats ground in a blender or food processor can be used to thicken soups or sauces or as a partial substitute for flour in baked goods.

fruited granola

3 cups quick oats
1 cup sliced almonds
1 cup honey
½ cup wheat germ or honey wheat germ
3 tablespoons butter, melted
1 teaspoon ground cinnamon
3 cups whole grain cereal flakes
½ cup dried blueberries or golden raisins
½ cup dried cranberries or cherries
½ cup dried banana chips or chopped pitted dates

1. Preheat oven to 325°F.

2. Spread oats and almonds in single layer in 13×9-inch baking pan. Bake 15 minutes or until lightly toasted, stirring frequently.

3. Combine honey, wheat germ, butter and cinnamon in large bowl until well blended. Add oats and almonds; toss to coat completely. Spread mixture in single layer in baking pan. Bake 20 minutes or until golden brown. Cool completely in pan on wire rack. Break mixture into chunks.

4. Combine oat chunks, cereal, blueberries, cranberries and banana chips in large bowl. Store in airtight container at room temperature up to 2 weeks. *Makes about 20 servings*

nutrients per serving:

Calories 210
Calories from Fat 30%
Protein 5g

Carbohydrate 36g
Fiber 4g
Total Fat 7g
Saturated Fat 2g
Cholesterol 5mg
Sodium 58mg

Olive Oil

Olive oil is a key ingredient in the healthy Mediterranean diet. While it is not lower in calories, it is much higher in flavor than ordinary vegetable oils.

benefits

Olive oil is a standard ingredient in diets for improving cholesterol levels, lowering blood pressure, minimizing diabetes complications and/or decreasing the risk of heart disease and cancer. All oils contain both saturated and unsaturated fats, but olive oil is considered healthy because it's very low in the saturated fats that tend to raise levels of LDL ("bad") cholesterol and high in monounsaturated fats. Substituting monounsaturated fats for saturated fats has been shown to not only lower LDL but also help raise HDL ("good") cholesterol. Extra virgin and virgin olive oils are also rich in flavonoids, antioxidant phytonutrients that help protect cells from damage that can lead to heart disease and cancer.

selection and storage

Extra virgin and virgin olive oils are from the first pressing of olives. Pure and light olive oils are more processed, lighter in flavor (but not calories) and usually less nutritious. Olive oil can become rancid from exposure to light and heat, so look for those sold in dark bottles, store them in a cool, dark area and use within a few months. For longer storage, refrigerate olive oil you won't use right away. It will become cloudy but return to normal at room temperature.

preparation and serving tips

Extra virgin olive oil isn't a good choice for high heat cooking since the delicate flavor that you paid a lot for will be compromised. Use it for salads, cold dishes and to add flavor after cooking. For a healthy substitute for butter, serve a shallow dish of good quality extra virgin olive oil for dipping with bread.

nutrients per serving:

Olive Oil
1 tablespoon

Calories 119
Protein 0g
Total Fat 13.5g
Saturated Fat 2g
Monounsaturated Fat 10g
Cholesterol 0mg
Carbohydrate 0g
Dietary Fiber 0g
Sodium 0mg
Vitamin E 1.9mg
Iron 0.1mg

quinoa and roasted corn

1 cup uncooked quinoa
2 cups water
½ teaspoon salt
4 ears corn *or* 2 cups frozen corn
¼ cup plus 1 tablespoon olive oil, divided
1 cup chopped green onions, divided
1 teaspoon coarse salt
1 cup quartered grape tomatoes or
    chopped plum tomatoes, drained*
1 cup black beans, rinsed and drained
¼ teaspoon grated lime peel
    Juice of 1 lime (about 2 tablespoons)
¼ teaspoon sugar
¼ teaspoon ground cumin
¼ teaspoon black pepper

Place tomatoes in fine-mesh strainer and place over bowl 10 to 15 minutes.

1. Place quinoa in fine-mesh strainer; rinse well under cold running water. Transfer to medium saucepan; add water and ½ teaspoon salt. Bring to a boil over high heat. Reduce heat; cover and simmer 15 to 18 minutes or until water is absorbed and quinoa is tender. Transfer to large bowl.

2. Meanwhile, remove husks and silk from corn; cut kernels off cobs. Heat ¼ cup oil in large skillet over medium-high heat. Add corn; cook 10 to 12 minutes or until tender and light brown, stirring occasionally. Stir in ⅔ cup green onions and coarse salt; cook and stir 2 minutes. Add corn to quinoa. Gently stir in tomatoes and black beans.

3. Combine lime peel, lime juice, sugar, cumin and black pepper in small bowl. Whisk in remaining 1 tablespoon oil until blended. Pour over quinoa mixture; toss lightly to coat. Sprinkle with remaining ⅓ cup green onions. Serve warm or chilled.

Makes 8 servings

nutrients per serving:

Calories 230
Calories from Fat 55%
Protein 7g
Carbohydrate 29g
Fiber 5g
Total Fat 11g
Saturated Fat 2g
Cholesterol 0mg
Sodium 250mg

Onions

Unassuming onions add flavor to so many dishes without having a starring role that we take them for granted. It's time to appreciate their contributions.

benefits

Onions share certain health benefits with their garlic cousins. They help lower blood cholesterol and reduce blood clotting, which together can help prevent the narrowing and eventual blockage of arteries that causes heart attacks and strokes. Onions also contain phytonutrients that fight inflammation, which a growing body of evidence suggests may contribute to a host of chronic diseases, from cancer and heart disease to arthritis, asthma and diabetes. One such phytonutrient, quercetin, may help relieve chronic prostatitis and has also shown anti-allergy and cancer-fighting properties in laboratory tests.

selection and storage

Onions come in dozens of shapes and colors. Choose firm, dry onions with shiny, tissue-thin skins. If they look discolored or have soft, wet spots, don't buy them. Onions keep three to four weeks stored in a dry, dark, cool location. Keep them away from potatoes, or a chemical reaction between the two will speed the spoilage of both. Look for green onions with crisp, not wilted, tops. Green onions should be refrigerated in an open plastic bag in the crisper drawer.

preparation and serving tips

There are many suggested methods to prevent tears while chopping onions, from wearing goggles to chilling the onion beforehand. Using a sharp knife so the onion cells are cut cleanly instead of being crushed helps. To get the onion smell off your hands, rub your fingers with lemon juice or vinegar. Sweet, red and green onions are ideal raw, while other onions are best cooked to mellow their flavor. You can sauté or roast onions with a small amount of oil or broth. Wash green onions, trim roots and remove the outer layer, then chop up bulb, stalk and all.

nutrients per serving:

Onions, white
½ cup raw chopped

Calories 32
Protein 1g
Total Fat 0g
Saturated Fat 0g
Cholesterol 0mg
Carbohydrate 8g
Dietary Fiber 1.5g
Sodium 0mg
Potassium 115mg
Calcium 18mg
Iron 0.2mg
Chromium 12mcg
Vitamin C 6mg
Folate 15mcg

balsamic beef, mushrooms and onions

2 large sweet onions, sliced
3 teaspoons olive oil, divided
½ teaspoon salt, divided
4 to 5 teaspoons balsamic vinegar, divided
3 ounces (about 1 cup) mushrooms, sliced
1 boneless beef top sirloin (about
1 pound), cut into ½-inch-thick slices
¼ teaspoon dried thyme
¼ to ½ teaspoon black pepper

1. Heat large nonstick skillet over medium heat. Add onions; cover and cook 15 minutes, stirring occasionally.

2. Stir in 2 teaspoons oil and ¼ teaspoon salt. Add 3 teaspoons vinegar, stirring and scraping up brown bits from bottom of skillet.

3. Reduce heat to medium-low. Add mushrooms; cook and stir 4 to 5 minutes or until mushrooms are soft. Remove vegetables from skillet and cover to keep warm.

4. Increase heat to medium-high. Add remaining 1 teaspoon oil and swirl to coat bottom of skillet. Add beef and sprinkle with remaining ¼ teaspoon salt, thyme and pepper. Cook 4 to 6 minutes or until desired doneness.

5. Remove from heat. Drizzle remaining 1 to 2 teaspoons vinegar over beef. Return vegetables to skillet and stir to combine.

Makes 4 servings

nutrients per serving:

Calories 216
Calories from Fat 38%
Protein 26g

Carbohydrate 7g
Fiber 1g
Total Fat 9g
Saturated Fat 2g
Cholesterol 53mg
Sodium 360mg

Oranges

How lucky we are to be able to enjoy sweet, juicy oranges year-round. In the 1800s oranges were so expensive they were considered a rare holiday treat.

nutrients per serving:

**Orange, navel
1 medium**

Calories 69
Protein 1g
Total Fat 0g
Saturated Fat 0g
Cholesterol 0mg
Carbohydrate 18g
Dietary Fiber 3g
Sodium 0mg
Potassium 230mg
Calcium 60mg
Iron 0.2mg
Vitamin A 346 IU
Vitamin C 83mg
Folate 48mcg

benefits

Oranges are best known for their abundant vitamin C. One orange provides 130 percent of the daily requirement for this antioxidant vitamin, which helps protect the heart and eyes, ward off infections, heal wounds and maintain healthy teeth, gums, skin, bones and blood vessels. Oranges also pack potassium for healthy blood pressure and folate to prevent certain birth defects. And an array of phytonutrients, some concentrated in the skin and pulp of the orange, offer protection from a host of common diseases and health problems.

selection and storage

California navels, with their thick skins and seedless flesh, are favorites for snacks. Valencias are the premier juice oranges. Blood oranges are somewhat smaller, extremely aromatic and have red streaks on their peel and running through their flesh. Mandarin oranges are small and sweet with thin, loose skins and easily sectioned segments; they're also available canned. Select firm fruit that are heavy for their size. Oranges that are part green or have brown patches can be just as ripe as those that are bright orange. Most varieties, except mandarins, will keep for two weeks in the refrigerator. Choose 100 percent orange juice without added sugar.

preparation and serving tips

For fruit salads and snacking, seedless oranges make things easier. Use orange juice in marinades, sauces and dressings. Or blend orange juice, bananas and low-fat yogurt for a delicious smoothie. Top a spinach salad with orange segments so the vitamin C can boost the absorption of iron in the spinach.

orange scallops with spinach and walnuts

- **¾ pound sea scallops**
- **½ cup orange juice**
- **2 tablespoons olive oil**
- **2 packages (8 ounces each) baby spinach**
- **2 tablespoons toasted walnuts**
  Salt and black pepper, to taste
- **1 can (11 ounces) mandarin oranges in juice, drained**

1. Rinse sea scallops and slice in half. Place in nonreactive dish and add orange juice. Stir well and set aside.

2. Heat oil in large skillet over medium heat. Cook spinach until wilted, stirring often.

3. Push spinach to edge of skillet. Increase heat to medium-high. Place scallops in center of skillet and cook 1 to 2 minutes or until opaque, turning once. Add walnuts and season with salt and pepper.

4. To serve, top spinach with scallops and mandarin orange segments; drizzle with pan juices. *Makes 4 servings*

nutrients per serving:

Calories 230
Calories from Fat 35%
Protein 14g
Carbohydrate 26g
Fiber 7g
Total Fat 9g
Saturated Fat 1g
Cholesterol 20mg
Sodium 520mg

Oregano

The word oregano is Greek for "joy of the mountain." In ancient times this herb was prescribed for many ailments and was also considered a good luck charm.

benefits

Whether fresh or dried, oregano is bursting with potent antioxidant nutrients. Indeed, it has one of the highest antioxidant levels of all herbs. Just 1 teaspoon of dried oregano has more antioxidants than a serving of almonds or asparagus, giving it serious disease-fighting potential. The specific medicinal effects associated with oregano are still being teased out but may include preventing the growth of cancerous cells and fighting the growth of bacteria and parasites that can cause ulcers and other gastrointestinal problems. Oregano is also a good source of lutein and zeaxanthin, phytonutrients that help prevent eye diseases common in older adults, such as cataracts and age-related macular degeneration.

selection and storage

Choose bright green bunches of fresh oregano with no trace of wilting or yellowing. Refrigerate it in a plastic bag for up to three days. Oregano is also easy to grow in the garden or in a pot on the windowsill. For best flavor and nutritional benefit, store dried oregano in a cool, dark place and use it within six months.

preparation and serving tips

Oregano is very aromatic and has a robust taste. Unlike some herbs, it retains much of its personality when dried. Oregano is traditional in Italian dishes, such as marinara sauce and pizza. It also enhances cheese and egg dishes and adds flavor to stews, soups and chilis. Oregano is part of many herb mixes, including Italian, Mexican and Greek seasoning blends. To substitute fresh oregano for dried, use 1 tablespoon of chopped fresh for each teaspoon of dried.

---

nutrients per serving:

**Oregano, dried
1 teaspoon**

Calories 3
Protein 0g
Total Fat 0g
Saturated Fat 0g
Cholesterol 0mg
Carbohydrate <1g
Dietary Fiber 0.5g
Sodium 0mg
Potassium 13mg
Calcium 16mg
Iron 0.4mg
Vitamin A 17 IU
Folate 2mcg

italian-style meat loaf

1 can (6 ounces) no-salt-added tomato
    paste
½ cup water
½ cup dry red wine
1 teaspoon minced garlic
1 teaspoon dried oregano
½ teaspoon dried basil
¼ teaspoon salt
¾ pound 95% lean ground beef
¾ pound 93% lean ground turkey
    breast
1 cup fresh whole wheat bread crumbs
    (2 slices whole wheat bread)
½ cup shredded zucchini
¼ cup cholesterol-free egg substitute

1. Preheat oven to 350°F. Combine tomato paste, water, wine, garlic, oregano, basil and salt in small saucepan. Bring to a boil; reduce heat to low. Simmer, uncovered, 15 minutes.

2. Combine beef, turkey, bread crumbs, zucchini, egg substitute and ½ cup tomato mixture in large bowl; mix lightly. Shape into loaf; place in ungreased 9×5-inch loaf pan.

3. Bake 45 minutes. Drain fat. Spread remaining tomato mixture over meat loaf. Bake 15 minutes or until cooked through (160°F). Cool 10 minutes before slicing.

Makes 8 servings

nutrients per serving:		
Calories 187	**Calories from Fat** 11%	**Total Fat** 6g
	Protein 19g	**Saturated Fat** 2g
	Carbohydrate 12g	**Cholesterol** 56mg
	Fiber 2g	**Sodium** 212mg

Papaya

Tropical papaya is an amazing fruit that can weigh up to 20 pounds and is used both green and ripe. When ripe, its golden flesh has a buttery consistency and a sweet, musky taste.

benefits

Papayas are bursting with vitamins A and C, antioxidants that help reduce heart disease and cancer risks. The generous dose of C also fortifies your body's wound-healing ability and helps keep your immune system in tip-top shape, so it can protect you from unhealthy invaders. In addition, papayas provide plenty of potassium, an essential mineral that helps keep blood pressure in a healthy range, and folate, a B vitamin needed during pregnancy to reduce the risk of birth defects. The fiber in papayas is mostly soluble, so it helps lower blood cholesterol.

selection and storage

The most commonly available papayas are grown in Hawaii; they are pear-shaped and weigh about a pound. Mexican papayas are much larger, longer and heavier. Look for papayas that have yellow to reddish orange skin and yield slightly to palm pressure. If they are slightly green, leave them at room temperature where they will ripen in a few days. Ripe fruit should be refrigerated and used as soon as possible. Unripe green papayas are usually cooked as a vegetable and have a different nutritional profile.

preparation and serving tips

Papayas should be washed, sliced lengthwise and the black seeds scooped out. The peppery seeds are edible though fairly bitter. Try papaya as a tropical breakfast treat with a squeeze of lime juice and a pinch of red pepper flakes. It is an excellent addition to salsa and makes an attractive, edible container for fruit salads.

nutrients per serving:

Papaya ½ medium			
	Total Fat 0g	Dietary Fiber 3g	Iron 0.4mg
	Saturated Fat 0g	Sodium 15mg	Vitamin A 1,492 IU
Calories 68	Cholesterol 0mg	Potassium 285mg	Vitamin C 96mg
Protein 1g	Carbohydrate 17g	Calcium 31mg	Folate 58mcg

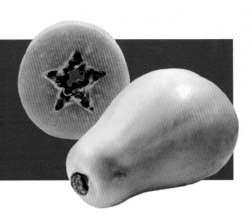

grilled red snapper with avocado-papaya salsa

- 1 teaspoon ground coriander
- 1 teaspoon paprika
- ¾ teaspoon salt
- ⅛ to ¼ teaspoon ground red pepper
- ½ cup diced ripe avocado
- ½ cup diced ripe papaya
- 2 tablespoons chopped fresh cilantro
- 1 tablespoon lime juice
- 1 tablespoon olive oil
- 4 skinless red snapper or halibut fillets (5 to 7 ounces each)
- 4 lime wedges

1. Oil grill grid. Prepare grill for direct cooking. Combine coriander, paprika, salt and red pepper in small bowl or cup; mix well.

2. For salsa, combine avocado, papaya, cilantro, lime juice and ¼ teaspoon spice mixture in medium bowl; set aside.

3. Brush oil over fish; sprinkle with remaining spice mixture. Grill fish, covered, over medium-high heat 10 minutes or until fish begins to flake when tested with fork, turning once. Serve with salsa and lime wedges.

Makes 4 servings

Parsnips

Parsnips are an underappreciated root vegetable. They look like beige carrots but are sweeter with a touch of the flavor of parsley, to which they are related.

benefits

Parsnips shine as a fiber source. They're high in soluble fiber, the type that helps lower blood cholesterol and keep blood sugar on an even keel. They're a good source of folate, a B vitamin that plays a role in reducing heart disease risk and preventing certain disabling birth defects. Parsnips also supply ample quantities of potassium, an aid to blood pressure control. But their pale color signals that, unlike their carrot cousins, parsnips lack beta-carotene.

selection and storage

Parsnips are available year-round in some markets, but peak season is late fall and winter. In fact, parsnips become sweeter if left in the ground until after a frost. Choose small- to medium-size parsnips that are firm, not limp. Large ones can be tough and often have a woody core. The beige skin should be fairly smooth, not shriveled, and without small roots.

Parsnips stored in a loosely closed plastic bag in your crisper drawer will keep for a couple of weeks.

preparation and serving tips

Scrub parsnips well before using and trim both ends. Scrape off or peel a thin layer of skin before cooking. The most flavorful way to enjoy parsnips is to cut them into chunks, coat them with a little olive oil and roast them in a hot oven (add carrots for extra color and nutrients, if you like). Parsnips can also be boiled and mashed like potatoes. Parsnips are great in soups and stews. Add them near the end of cooking time so they do not become mushy.

roasted root vegetables with miso-peanut dressing

1 pound carrots, peeled and cut into
    1-inch pieces
1 pound parsnips, peeled and cut into
    1-inch pieces
¼ teaspoon salt
¼ teaspoon black pepper
¼ cup plain soymilk
3 tablespoons natural peanut butter
2 tablespoons mild miso*
1 tablespoon honey

*Miso, which resembles peanut butter, is a paste
made from fermented soybeans. It is an essential
element of Japanese cooking and comes in many
colors and flavors. Generally, the lighter the color
the milder the flavor. Miso can be found in Asian
and natural foods stores.

1. Preheat oven to 400°F. Spray large roasting pan
with nonstick cooking spray.

2. Place carrots and parsnips in single layer in
prepared pan. Sprinkle with salt and pepper.
Bake 30 to 40 minutes or until tender, stirring
occasionally.

3. Whisk soymilk, peanut butter, miso and honey
in small bowl. Drizzle sauce over vegetables or
serve on the side as dipping sauce.

Makes 6 servings

nutrients per serving:

Calories 155
Calories from Fat 28%
Protein 4g
Carbohydrate 24g
Fiber 6g
Total Fat 5g
Saturated Fat <1g
Cholesterol 0mg
Sodium 394mg

125

Pasta

Nothing could be simpler than pasta. It's just flour, water and sometimes eggs. But there's nothing simple about the hundreds of shapes and millions of delicious ways to enjoy it.

benefits

Pasta offers complex carbohydrates for sustained energy plus the B vitamins the body needs to help turn those carbs into fuel. That fuel comes with few calories, unless you add a rich, fat-laden sauce. By selecting a whole wheat or whole grain pasta, you get the additional minerals and fiber that would be lost during refining—and you get an even more satisfying and health-enhancing meal. If the pasta is fortified with a vegetable fiber called inulin, it can even help reduce your blood cholesterol and blood sugar levels.

selection and storage

Look for products labeled whole wheat or whole grain. Pasta made from whole wheat is darker in color and has a nutty, hearty flavor. Whole grain pastas include wheat plus other ingredients, such as oats, barley, flax and legumes, to boost fiber and nutrients. Unopened packages of dried pasta will keep in your cupboard for a year or more. Once opened, transfer the contents to an airtight container or sealed food storage bag.

preparation and serving tips

To cook pasta, bring an abundant quantity of salted water to a rolling boil. Add the pasta and stir once or twice. Boil, uncovered, until it's al dente—tender but firm. The time it takes will vary based on the kind and amount of pasta. Don't always believe the package directions. The best test is to remove a piece, quickly cool it and taste. Drain pasta immediately, and remember that it will continue to cook a bit even after draining.

nutrients per serving:

**Pasta, whole wheat
½ cup cooked**

Calories 87
Protein 3.5g
Total Fat 0g
Saturated Fat 0g
Cholesterol 0mg
Carbohydrate 19g
Dietary Fiber 3g
Sodium 0mg
Potassium 30mg
Calcium 10mg
Iron 0.7mg
Selenium 18mcg
Vitamin A 2 IU
Folate 4mcg

enlightened macaroni and cheese

8 ounces uncooked rotini pasta or elbow
    macaroni
1 tablespoon all-purpose flour
2 teaspoons cornstarch
¼ teaspoon dry mustard
1 can (12 ounces) evaporated fat-free milk
1 cup (4 ounces) shredded reduced-fat
    sharp Cheddar cheese
½ cup (2 ounces) shredded reduced-fat
    Monterey Jack cheese
1 jar (2 ounces) diced pimiento, drained
    and rinsed
1 teaspoon Worcestershire sauce
¼ teaspoon black pepper
1 tablespoon plain dry bread crumbs
1 tablespoon paprika

1. Preheat oven to 375°F.

2. Cook pasta according to package
directions. Drain and set aside.

3. Combine flour, cornstarch and mustard in
medium saucepan; stir in evaporated milk
until smooth. Cook and stir over low heat
about 8 minutes or until slightly thickened.

4. Remove from heat; stir in cheeses,
pimiento, Worcestershire sauce and pepper.
Add pasta; mix well.

5. Spray 1½-quart casserole with nonstick
cooking spray. Spoon mixture into casserole;
sprinkle with bread crumbs and paprika.

6. Bake 20 minutes or until bubbly and
heated through. *Makes 6 servings*

nutrients per serving:

Calories 266
Calories from Fat 19%
Protein 18g
Carbohydrate 35g
Fiber 2g
Total Fat 6g
Saturated Fat 3g
Cholesterol 18mg
Sodium 200mg

Peanuts

What would we do without peanuts? Imagine no more PB&J sandwiches or sacks of peanuts at the ball game! The versatile peanut is actually a legume, not a true nut, but that doesn't make it less delicious or wholesome.

benefits

Peanuts possess a variety of healthy components, including monounsaturated fats for the heart and protein for building infection-fighting antibodies. Arginine, an amino acid that appears to improve blood flow to the brain, heart and other organs and may help treat high blood pressure and erectile dysfunction, is also present. The list goes on, including fiber to lower blood cholesterol and improve digestion and phytonutrients such as resveratrol. Vitamin E and selenium, powerful antioxidants, help battle cell damage and inflammation that can lead to heart disease, cancer and Alzheimer's.

selection and storage

When buying whole peanuts in their shells, take a sniff. They should not smell musty or rancid. If the peanut rattles when you shake the shell, it's dried out and not as fresh as it should be. Shelled peanuts are available in vacuum-sealed containers and are usually roasted and sometimes salted. Natural peanut butter is unprocessed and the oil may separate out. Simply stir to combine and refrigerate. Check ingredient lists, since many peanut butters contain sugar or other additives. Natural peanut butter stored in the refrigerator will remain fresh about six months.

preparation and serving tips

Enjoy nutritious peanuts as a snack, but keep your portion to about 1 ounce, or a small handful. Sprinkle peanuts on salads or stir-fries for crunch and flavor. Peanut butter has many uses besides sandwiches. Enjoy it as a snack spread on apple wedges, crackers or toast.

nutrients per serving:

**Peanuts, dry roasted without salt
1 ounce**

Calories 166
Protein 7g
Total Fat 14g
Saturated Fat 2g
Cholesterol 0mg
Carbohydrate 6g
Dietary Fiber 2.5g
Sodium 0mg
Potassium 185mg
Calcium 15mg
Iron 0.6mg
Magnesium 50mg
Phosphorus 101mg
Selenium 2.1mcg
Folate 41mcg
Vitamin E 2mg

peanut butter cereal bars

- 3 cups mini marshmallows
- 3 tablespoons butter
- ½ cup reduced-fat peanut butter
- 3½ cups crisp rice cereal
- 1 cup quick oats
- ⅓ cup mini semisweet chocolate chips

Microwave Directions

1. Spray 13×9-inch baking pan with nonstick cooking spray.

2. Combine marshmallows and butter in large microwavable bowl. Microwave on HIGH 15 seconds; stir. Microwave 1 minute; stir until marshmallows are melted and mixture is smooth.

3. Add peanut butter; stir. Add cereal and oats; stir until well coated. Spread into prepared pan. Immediately sprinkle chocolate chips on top; lightly press. Cool completely in pan.   *Makes 40 servings*

Tip: To make spreading the cereal mixture easier and cleanup a snap, lightly spray your spoon with nonstick cooking spray before stirring these bars.

nutrients per serving:

Calories 66
Calories from Fat 36%
Protein 1g
Carbohydrate 10g
Fiber 1g
Total Fat 3g
Saturated Fat 1g
Cholesterol 2mg
Sodium 54mg

Pears

Let's praise the pear! It's in season all winter, comes in a stunning variety of colors and can be enjoyed as is or turned into a dessert, a snack, a salad or a smoothie.

benefits

The amount of fiber in other fruit pales in comparison to that in a pear. Its gritty insoluble fiber is good for preventing and treating digestive woes, such as constipation and hemorrhoids, and may help protect against cancerous colon growths. Enough of its fiber is soluble, though, that it can also help lower blood cholesterol and blunt blood sugar spikes. Pears provide decent amounts of heart-healthy potassium, vitamin C and folate, too.

nutrients per serving:

Pear
1 medium

Calories 103
Protein 1g
Total Fat 0g
Saturated Fat 0g
Cholesterol 0mg
Carbohydrate 28g
Dietary Fiber 5.5g
Sodium 0mg
Potassium 210mg
Calcium 16mg
Iron 0.3mg
Vitamin A 41 IU
Vitamin C 8mg
Folate 12mcg

selection and storage

Bartletts are the most common variety, fresh or canned. Anjou pears have a firmer, denser flesh and are not quite as sweet. Both Bartletts and Anjous also have red varieties. Boscs, which have elongated necks and a russet brown color, are crunchy; Comice pears are plump and sweet with a custardy texture. Pears are one of the only fruits that become sweeter and tastier after picking. Buy them when firm and let them ripen on the counter until they yield to gentle pressure. Canned pears have more calories when packed in syrup and less fiber without their skins.

preparation and serving tips

To get a pear's full nutritional value, eat the skin. Of course, wash it well first. Slice ripe red Bartletts or Anjous into salads for color and flavor. Pears are great mixed with nonfat yogurt and cereal for a quick breakfast. Firm pears, like Bosc, are good for cooking. The traditional method is poaching in wine or juice, but pears can also be baked or sautéed with a sprinkle of brown sugar.

cinnamon pear crisp

- 8 pears, peeled and sliced
- ¾ cup unsweetened apple juice concentrate
- ½ cup golden raisins
- ¼ cup plus 3 tablespoons all-purpose flour, divided
- 1 teaspoon ground cinnamon
- ⅓ cup quick oats
- 3 tablespoons packed dark brown sugar
- 3 tablespoons margarine, melted

1. Preheat oven to 375°F. Spray 11×7-inch baking dish with nonstick cooking spray.

2. Combine pears, apple juice concentrate, raisins, 3 tablespoons flour and cinnamon in large bowl; mix well. Transfer to prepared baking dish.

3. Combine oats, remaining ¼ cup flour, brown sugar and margarine in medium bowl; stir until mixture resembles coarse crumbs. Sprinkle evenly over pear mixture. Bake 1 hour or until golden brown. Cool in pan on wire rack.   *Makes 12 servings*

nutrients per serving:

Calories 179
Calories from Fat 17%
Protein 2g

Carbohydrate 38g
Fiber 3g
Total Fat 4g
Saturated Fat 1g
Cholesterol 0mg
Sodium 40mg

Pecans

Nutrient-dense pecans are native to North America. Enjoy the rich, satisfying taste that made pecans an important part of the diet of Native Americans and our founding fathers, including George Washington.

benefits

A fistful of pecans packs a potent punch of disease-fighting nutrients. Antioxidant vitamin E is thought to protect the heart; potassium, calcium and magnesium promote healthy blood pressure. An ounce of pecans (about 19 halves) provides about 10 percent of daily fiber and zinc needs. Fiber, of course, is nature's broom, helping to keep you comfortably regular. And zinc is essential for immunity and wound healing. Plus, studies have shown that including just 1 or 2 ounces of pecans daily in a heart-healthy diet can reduce LDL ("bad") cholesterol and increase HDL ("good") cholesterol.

selection and storage

Shelled pecans are available as halves, chips or ground. They may be raw, dry or oil roasted and salted or unsalted. Unsalted raw pecans are usually used in recipes, while roasted varieties are used for snacking; choose unsalted, dry roasted for fewer calories and less sodium. Shelled pecans can be kept up to nine months if refrigerated or about three months when stored in a cool, dry place. Unshelled pecans can be stored for three to six months in a cool, dry place.

preparation and serving tips

To bring out the flavor of raw pecans, toast them in a 350°F oven for 5 to 7 minutes or until lightly browned, stirring occasionally. Use them as a topping for salads, vegetables and cereal. Pecans add flavor and crunch to baked goods like cookies, muffins and pancakes, and ground pecans can be used as a high-protein, low-carb breading for chicken or fish.

savory bread stuffing

- 2 teaspoons canola oil
- ½ cup chopped onion
- ½ cup chopped celery
- 1 cup fat-free reduced-sodium chicken broth
- ½ cup unsweetened apple juice
- 4 cups (7 ounces) seasoned cubed bread stuffing mix
- ¾ cup diced unpeeled red apple
- ¼ cup chopped pecans, toasted*

*To toast pecans, spread in single layer on baking sheet. Bake in preheated 350°F oven 5 to 7 minutes or until golden brown, stirring occasionally.

1. Preheat oven to 350°F. Spray 2½-quart casserole with nonstick cooking spray.

2. Heat oil in medium saucepan over medium heat. Add onion and celery; cook and stir 7 to 8 minutes or until vegetables are tender and lightly browned. Stir in broth and juice; bring to a boil over high heat. Remove from heat. Stir in stuffing mix, apple and pecans; mix well. Transfer to prepared casserole.

3. Cover and bake 30 to 35 minutes or until heated through.   *Makes 12 servings*

nutrients per serving:

Calories 111
Calories from Fat 25%
Protein 3g

Carbohydrate 18g
Fiber 2g
Total Fat 3g
Saturated Fat <1g
Cholesterol 0mg
Sodium 317mg

Pineapple

Serve fresh pineapple for dessert and no one will complain about missing sweets. Pineapple gets high scores for its unique sweet and tart taste, fiber content and health benefits.

benefits

Pineapple is a sweet trove of nutrients. A ½ cup offers more than a third of your daily requirement for vitamin C, which helps keep your immune system in tip-top shape for resisting colds, flu and other infectious diseases. One cup provides more than the recommended daily intake of manganese, a mineral essential for energy production and strong bones. This tropical treat also supplies decent amounts of copper, needed for proper brain and nerve function, and folate for preventing certain birth defects. Fresh, raw pineapple contains the enzyme bromelain, a digestive aid that also helps prevent inflammation and swelling.

selection and storage

When choosing a pineapple, let your nose be your guide. Sniff the bottom of the pineapple; it should smell sweet and fresh. If it smells fermented and sickly sweet, the fruit is deteriorating. Pineapples begin to ripen from the bottom, so choose one that is golden yellow at least at its base. A completely green pineapple will never ripen. The flesh should yield slightly when pressed. Choose canned pineapple in juice or water, not syrup.

preparation and serving tips

To tackle a pineapple, cut off a slice at the bottom and top. Stand the pineapple upright on a cutting board and use a sharp knife to cut the skin off. Remove any remaining eyes with the tip of a knife or vegetable peeler. Lay the pineapple down and slice it into rounds. Or for chunks, cut the whole peeled pineapple into quarters, then cut away the tough core at the pointy end of each quarter and chop the pineapple. Try grilling fresh pineapple slices for an elegant side dish or dessert. Use pineapple chunks in fruit salads or make kabobs with other in-season fruits.

nutrients per serving:

Pineapple
½ cup raw

Calories 41
Protein 1g
Total Fat 0g
Saturated Fat 0g
Cholesterol 0mg
Carbohydrate 11g
Dietary Fiber 1g
Sodium 0mg
Potassium 90mg
Calcium 11mg
Copper 100mcg
Manganese 0.8mg
Zinc 0.1mg
Vitamin C 39mg
Folate 15mcg

caramelized pineapple

1 tablespoon stick margarine
2 cups fresh pineapple chunks
3 tablespoons sugar
¾ cup vanilla reduced-fat frozen yogurt

1. Spray baking sheet with nonstick cooking spray.

2. Melt margarine in large nonstick skillet over medium-high heat. Mix pineapple chunks and sugar in skillet; cook and stir about 7 minutes or until beginning to brown. Cook 2 to 4 minutes more or until caramelized, stirring and turning pineapple occasionally. Spread on prepared baking sheet. Cool 5 minutes.

3. Spoon pineapple into four dessert dishes and top with frozen yogurt. Serve immediately.   *Makes 4 servings*

nutrients per serving:

Calories 145
Calories from Fat 25%
Protein 2g
Carbohydrate 28g
Fiber 1g
Total Fat 4g
Saturated Fat 1g
Cholesterol 4mg
Sodium 52mg

Pistachios

Pistachios almost look like they're smiling; in fact, they are known as the happy nut in China. Fun to eat as a snack, pistachios also make healthy additions to savory or sweet recipes.

benefits

In a nutshell, pistachios pack a powerful punch against heart disease. They are tops when it comes to phytosterols, which compete with cholesterol in the body for absorption, helping to reduce cholesterol levels in the blood. They contain arginine, an amino acid that helps improve circulation by dilating blood vessels. Pistachios are rich in monounsaturated fats, the same heart-healthy fats found in olive oil. You also get a hefty amount of resveratrol, a phytonutrient found in wine that may play a role in fighting cancer and heart disease. That's not to mention the noteworthy amounts of potassium, magnesium, copper, vitamin B$_6$ and vitamin E.

selection and storage

Unshelled pistachios should have the shells partly opened, which shows that the nut is mature and ready to eat. The nutmeats are pale green and the shells are naturally beige. Pistachios with bright red or stark white shells have been artificially colored.

Shelled pistachios are more expensive but convenient for recipe use. Store pistachios in an airtight container in the refrigerator for up to three months or in the freezer for up to one year.

preparation and serving tips

Part of the fun of eating pistachios is extracting them from their shells, which also helps slow you down so you're less likely to overdo it. Pistachios work well in sweet or savory dishes. A handful of toasted pistachios can add a delicious (and attractive) accent to vegetable or rice dishes. Sprinkle a handful of chopped pistachios on salads, or bake them into muffins, pancakes or cookies.

nutrients per serving:

Pistachios, dry roasted without salt
1 ounce

Calories 161
Protein 6g
Total Fat 13g
Saturated Fat 1.5g
Cholesterol 0mg
Carbohydrate 8g
Dietary Fiber 3g
Sodium 0mg
Potassium 285mg
Calcium 30mg
Iron 1.1mg
Vitamin A 73 IU
Vitamin C 1mg
Folate 14mcg
Magnesium 31mg
Vitamin E 0.7mg

Pomegranate

The jewel-like interior of a pomegranate is almost too beautiful to eat, but don't let that stop you. Those sparkling little seeds and their juice are loaded with nutrients.

benefits

Pomegranates offer up plenty of potassium, a mineral that plays an important role in balancing fluids in the body and helps maintain a steady heartbeat as it lowers blood pressure. When you eat the seeds, you'll get fiber that helps keep you regular. Pomegranate juice is rich in disease-fighting antioxidants, with close to three times the antioxidants as green tea or red wine. Pomegranate juice may help reduce the buildup of artery-clogging plaque, lower levels of LDL ("bad") cholesterol and help improve blood flow.

selection and storage

Fresh pomegranates are at their best in late fall and early winter. Choose a fresh pomegranate with a bright, deep red color and unblemished skin that feels heavy for its size. Refrigerate for up to two months or store in a cool, dark place for up to a month. Once cut, seeds can be refrigerated for about three days or frozen. Pomegranate juice is available in bottles, as concentrate or in combination with other juices.

preparation and serving tips

Eating a fresh pomegranate is a delightfully messy business and the juice stains, so dress accordingly. Cut the pomegranate in pieces and pry out the seeds. The membrane that holds them is bitter and shouldn't be eaten. A neater method is to pry off the seeds while the pieces are immersed in a bowl of cold water; the membrane will float to the top. Pomegranate seeds make a gorgeous garnish, and the juice can be used in marinades and sauces.

Pork Tenderloin

Pork tenderloin is comparable to skinless chicken breast in calories and fat, but higher in other nutrients. It works with almost any flavor profile, cooks quickly and turns out tender.

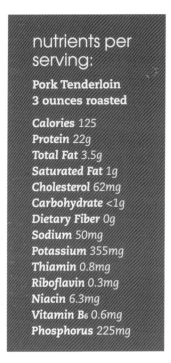

nutrients per serving:

**Pork Tenderloin
3 ounces roasted**

Calories 125
Protein 22g
Total Fat 3.5g
Saturated Fat 1g
Cholesterol 62mg
Carbohydrate <1g
Dietary Fiber 0g
Sodium 50mg
Potassium 355mg
Thiamin 0.8mg
Riboflavin 0.3mg
Niacin 6.3mg
Vitamin B6 0.6mg
Phosphorus 225mg

benefits

Besides qualifying as an "extra lean" meat, a serving of pork tenderloin provides more than 20 percent of your daily needs for thiamin, niacin, riboflavin, vitamin B6, phosphorus and protein and at least 10 percent of zinc and potassium. Among meats, pork is highest in thiamin, an essential vitamin that works with other B vitamins to convert food into energy. Its phosphorus is essential for strong bones and teeth, while zinc helps with wound healing and your ability to taste and smell. Pork tenderloin is even lower in cholesterol than a skinless chicken breast, an important quality for a heart-healthy diet.

selection and storage

Pork tenderloin is long and thin and easy to find in the fresh meat section of the supermarket. A tenderloin weighs between ¾ and 1½ pounds. Figure about 4 ounces raw to yield a 3-ounce cooked serving per person. Fresh pork tenderloin can be stored in the refrigerator three to five days or frozen for up to six months.

preparation and serving tips

Pork tenderloin makes an elegant entrée for a dinner party but cooks quickly enough for a weeknight meal. It has a mild flavor, so it's best when prepared with a spice rub, marinade, stuffing or flavorful sauce. To keep the tenderloin juicy, be careful not to overcook it. A meat thermometer should read 160°F and the meat should be barely pink in the center.

rosemary roast pork tenderloin and vegetables

¼ cup reduced-sodium chicken broth

1 tablespoon olive or vegetable oil

3 large parsnips, peeled and cut diagonally into ½-inch slices

2 cups baby carrots

1 red bell pepper, cut into ¾-inch pieces

1 medium sweet or yellow onion, cut into wedges

2 small pork tenderloins (12 ounces each)

2 tablespoons Dijon or spicy Dijon mustard

2 teaspoons dried rosemary

¾ teaspoon salt (optional)

½ teaspoon black pepper

1. Preheat oven to 400°F. Spray large shallow roasting pan or jelly-roll pan with nonstick cooking spray.

2. Combine broth and oil in small bowl. Combine parsnips, carrots and 3 tablespoons broth mixture in prepared pan; toss to coat. Roast 10 minutes.

3. Add bell pepper, onion and remaining broth mixture to pan; toss to coat. Push vegetables to edges of pan. Place pork in center of pan; spread with mustard. Sprinkle pork and vegetables with rosemary, salt, if desired, and black pepper.

4. Roast 25 to 30 minutes or until vegetables are tender and pork is barely pink in center (160°F). Transfer pork to cutting board; tent with foil and let stand 5 minutes. Cut pork crosswise into ½-inch slices; serve with vegetables and any juices from pan. *Makes 6 servings*

nutrients per serving:

Calories 230
Calories from Fat 35%
Protein 14g

Carbohydrate 26g
Fiber 7g
Total Fat 9g
Saturated Fat 1g
Cholesterol 20mg
Sodium 520mg

Potatoes

America's favorite vegetable is an economical, versatile, delicious way to get important nutrition. (Just skip the fries and go easy on the butter!)

benefits

Potatoes are loaded with vitamin C, and with the skin on, a medium potato supplies more than 25 percent of your daily needs for blood pressure-lowering potassium—twice as much as a banana. The fiber you get from eating a potato and its skin is a mix of soluble and insoluble, so it helps to keep you regular and lower cholesterol.

nutrients per serving:

**Potato
1 medium baked**

Calories 161
Protein 4g
Total Fat 0g
Saturated Fat 0g
Cholesterol 0mg
Carbohydrate 37g
Dietary Fiber 4g
Sodium 15mg
Potassium 925mg
Calcium 26mg
Iron 1.9mg
Vitamin A 17 IU
Vitamin C 17mg
Folate 48mcg

selection and storage

There are hundreds of varieties of potatoes, including those with blue flesh. Russets are considered best for baking or mashing because of their fluffy, starchy interior. For recipes where a potato needs to hold its shape, choose a waxy variety like round red or white. New potatoes are young potatoes of any variety; fingerlings are cute thumb-sized potatoes from heritage types. Choose firm potatoes without green spots or sprouts. Store mature potatoes in a dry, cool, dark, ventilated location for up to two weeks. New potatoes only last about a week.

preparation and serving tips

Just before cooking, scrub potatoes well with a vegetable brush and cut away sprouts or bad spots. A greenish tinge usually means a potato has been exposed to light and should be avoided. (The green is solanine, which is poisonous in large quantities.) Potatoes take well to any cooking method. Try roasting or grilling, especially for quick-cooking fingerlings or new potatoes. The microwave makes baked potatoes in a matter of minutes and is a time-saving jump start for potatoes that you wish to finish in the sauté pan or on the grill.

herbed potato chips

Nonstick cooking spray
2 unpeeled medium red potatoes
   (about ½ pound)
1 tablespoon olive oil
2 tablespoons minced fresh dill, thyme
   or rosemary leaves *or* 2 teaspoons
   dried dill weed, thyme or rosemary
¼ teaspoon garlic salt
⅛ teaspoon black pepper
1¼ cups fat-free sour cream

1. Preheat oven to 450°F. Spray baking sheets with cooking spray.

2. Cut potatoes crosswise into very thin slices, about 1/16 inch thick. Pat dry with paper towels. Arrange potato slices in single layer on prepared baking sheets; coat potatoes with cooking spray.

3. Bake 10 minutes; turn slices over. Brush with oil. Combine dill, garlic salt and pepper in small bowl; sprinkle evenly onto potato slices. Bake 5 to 10 minutes or until potatoes are golden brown. Cool on baking sheets. Serve with sour cream.

Makes 6 servings

nutrients per serving:

Calories 106

Calories from Fat 17%
Protein 4g
Carbohydrate 16g
Fiber 1g

Total Fat 2g
Saturated Fat <1g
Cholesterol 8mg
Sodium 84mg

Prunes

Pity the poor prune known mostly as a remedy for constipation. The luscious dried plum (its new name) is a delightful snack and ingredient in dishes both sweet and savory.

benefits

Prunes are a sweet way to add laxative fiber to your diet; a single prune contains more than half a gram of fiber. Prunes also contain the natural laxative diphenylisatin, which is why prune juice can also help relieve constipation. Prunes' soluble fiber helps lower cholesterol levels. Prunes are rich in disease-fighting antioxidants, including beta-carotene, and in blood pressure-lowering potassium along with magnesium. Prunes are also a source of iron and can help prevent iron-deficiency anemia.

selection and storage

If the last time you had a prune it was tough, dry and had a pit, you're in for a surprise. Most prunes are now available pitted and they even come flavored with orange, lemon and other fruit essences. After opening the package, reseal well or transfer the prunes to an airtight container or plastic bag. Stored in a cool, dry location or in the refrigerator, they'll keep for up to a year.

preparation and serving tips

Enjoy prunes as a fat-free snack or combine them with other dried fruits, nuts and seeds for a healthy trail mix. Add chopped prunes to cereal, yogurt or salads. They can also add a touch of sweetness to savory dishes, including pot roasts and stews, and grain-based dishes like couscous. Puréed prunes can also be used as a fat substitute in baked goods. To replace butter, use half as much prune purée. This works best in recipes with complementary flavors and a dark color, chocolate being a good example.

nutrients per serving:

Prunes
¼ cup

Calories 104
Protein 1g

Total Fat 0g
Saturated Fat 0g
Cholesterol 0mg
Carbohydrate 28g

Dietary Fiber 3g
Sodium 0mg
Potassium 320mg
Calcium 19mg

Iron 0.4mg
Vitamin A 340 IU
Magnesium 16mg
Folate 2mcg

no-guilt chocolate brownies

- 1 cup semisweet chocolate chips
- ¼ cup packed brown sugar
- 2 tablespoons granulated sugar
- ½ teaspoon baking powder
- ¼ teaspoon salt
- ½ cup cholesterol-free egg substitute
- 1 jar (2½ ounces) baby food prunes
- 1 teaspoon vanilla
- 1 cup old-fashioned oats
- ⅓ cup nonfat dry milk powder
- ¼ cup all-purpose flour
- 2 teaspoons powdered sugar

1. Preheat oven to 350°F. Spray 8-inch square baking pan with nonstick cooking spray. Melt chips in top of double boiler over simmering water.

2. Combine brown sugar, granulated sugar, baking powder and salt in large bowl. Add egg substitute, prunes and vanilla; beat with electric mixer at medium speed 2 minutes or until well blended. Stir in oats, milk powder, flour and melted chocolate.

3. Pour batter into prepared pan. Bake 30 minutes or until toothpick inserted in center comes out clean. Cool completely in pan on wire rack. Dust with powdered sugar before serving. *Makes 16 servings*

Pumpkin

Pumpkin is good for a lot more than pie and jack-o'-lanterns. Native Americans roasted, baked, boiled and dried it. From soup to seeds, pumpkin makes great eats.

nutrients per serving:

Pumpkin
½ cup cooked

Calories 24
Protein 1g
Total Fat 0g
Saturated Fat 0g
Cholesterol 0mg
Carbohydrate 6g
Dietary Fiber 1.5g
Sodium 0mg
Potassium 280mg
Calcium 18mg
Iron 0.7mg
Vitamin A 6,115 IU
Vitamin C 6mg
Folate 11mcg

benefits

The bright orange color clearly indicates that pumpkin is an excellent source of that all-important antioxidant beta-carotene. Research shows that people who eat a diet rich in beta-carotene are less likely to develop certain cancers than those who fail to include beta-carotene-rich foods in their diet. Pumpkin is also a good low-calorie source of iron and potassium and provides a decent amount of fiber.

selection and storage

The field pumpkin we buy for Halloween is prized for its size and hollow interior. Cooking pumpkins are smaller and yield denser and much tastier flesh. Look for varieties with "pie" or "sugar" in their names. A whole pumpkin keeps well for up to a month if stored in a cool, dry spot. Cooked pumpkin freezes well and will last up to a year. Canned pumpkin is available year-round and is about as nutritious as fresh, but be aware that pumpkin pie filling has added sugar and spices and cannot be used interchangeably.

preparation and serving tips

The easiest way to turn fresh pumpkin into purée is to cut it in half and remove the stringy pulp. Separate and save the seeds to roast. Bake the pumpkin halves for 1 hour or until tender, scoop out the softened flesh and mash or purée it. Freeze any purée you won't use immediately. You can also peel pumpkin and cut it into chunks to boil or microwave. Pumpkin can be turned into soups, puddings, cookies, quick breads and, of course, pies.

cinnamon sugared pumpkin-pecan muffins

8 tablespoons sugar, divided
3 teaspoons ground cinnamon, divided
1 cup 100% bran cereal
1 cup fat-free (skim) milk
1 cup all-purpose flour
1 tablespoon baking powder
½ teaspoon baking soda
½ teaspoon salt
1 cup solid-pack pumpkin
1 egg, beaten
1 tablespoon vanilla
1 package (2 ounces) pecan chips
   (½ cup)

1. Preheat oven to 400°F. Spray 12 standard (2½-inch) nonstick muffin cups with nonstick cooking spray. Combine 2 tablespoons sugar and 1 teaspoon cinnamon in small bowl for topping; set aside.

2. Combine cereal and milk in large bowl; let stand 5 minutes to soften. Meanwhile, combine flour, remaining 6 tablespoons sugar, baking powder, remaining 2 teaspoons cinnamon, baking soda and salt in large bowl; mix well.

3. Whisk pumpkin, egg and vanilla into cereal mixture. Gently fold in flour mixture just until blended. *Do not overmix.* Spoon equal amounts of batter into prepared muffin cups; sprinkle evenly with pecan chips. Sprinkle with cinnamon-sugar topping.

4. Bake 20 to 25 minutes or until toothpick inserted into centers comes out clean. Cool in pan 3 minutes. Remove to wire rack. Serve warm or at room temperature.   *Makes 12 servings*

nutrients per serving:

Calories 141
Calories from Fat 25%
Protein 4g
Carbohydrate 24g
Fiber 3g
Total Fat 4g
Saturated Fat <1g
Cholesterol 18mg
Sodium 335mg

Pumpkin Seeds

Don't forget to save the seeds when cleaning your pumpkin. Toasted, they make a great low-calorie, fiber-rich snack. When there's no pumpkin handy, go for pepitas, which are simply hulled pumpkin seeds.

benefits

Pumpkin seeds are a rich source of protein, providing about 6 grams per ounce—almost as much as an equal serving of peanuts—but with less fat and more fiber (when you eat the hulls). They also supply a decent amount of iron, important for maintaining oxygen-carrying hemoglobin in red blood cells. The healthy unsaturated fat in pumpkin seeds helps keep blood cholesterol levels from rising, and the magnesium and potassium play important roles in muscle contraction, blood clotting and regulating blood pressure.

selection and storage

Pumpkin seeds can be purchased with or without the white hull, roasted or raw, salted or unsalted. Dry roasted is the healthiest option. Pale green pepitas can be found in the Mexican food section of the supermarket or at Latin American markets. Pumpkin seeds can be stored in an airtight container in a cool, dark place for several months. If they develop an off odor they should be discarded.

preparation and serving tips

To roast fresh pumpkin seeds, scoop them out and separate from the stringy fibers. Rinse them and let dry, then bake on an oiled baking sheet at 350°F for 20 minutes or until crisp. Lightly salt them and add chili powder or other seasonings. Enjoy them as a snack or add them to trail mix. Pepitas can be sprinkled on soups and salads or baked into breads and cookies. Pepitas are a popular ingredient in Mexican cooking, where they are often ground and used to thicken and flavor sauces.

nutrients per serving:

Pumpkin Seeds, unhulled, dry roasted without salt
½ ounce

Calories 63
Protein 3g
Total Fat 3g
Saturated Fat 0.5g
Cholesterol 0mg
Carbohydrate 8g
Dietary Fiber 2.5g
Sodium 0mg
Potassium 130mg
Calcium 8mg
Iron 0.5mg
Vitamin A 9 IU
Folate 1mcg
Magnesium 37mg

chickpea-vegetable soup

Nonstick cooking spray
1 cup chopped onion
½ cup chopped green bell pepper
2 cloves garlic, minced
1 teaspoon olive oil
2 cans (about 14 ounces each)
    no-salt-added tomatoes, cut up
    and undrained
3 cups water
2 cups broccoli florets
1 can (about 15 ounces) chickpeas,
    rinsed, drained and slightly mashed
½ cup (3 ounces) uncooked orzo pasta
1 bay leaf
1 tablespoon chopped fresh thyme *or*
    1 teaspoon dried thyme
1 tablespoon chopped fresh rosemary
    leaves *or* 1 teaspoon dried rosemary
1 tablespoon lime juice or lemon juice
½ teaspoon ground turmeric
¼ teaspoon salt
¼ teaspoon ground red pepper
¼ cup toasted pumpkin seeds

1. Spray large saucepan with cooking spray; heat over medium heat. Add onion, bell pepper, garlic and oil; cook and stir until vegetables are tender.

2. Add tomatoes with juice, water, broccoli, chickpeas, orzo, bay leaf, thyme, rosemary, lime juice, turmeric, salt and red pepper. Bring to a boil over high heat. Reduce heat to medium-low; cover and simmer 10 to 12 minutes or until orzo is tender.

3. Remove bay leaf. Ladle soup into four bowls. Sprinkle with pumpkin seeds.

Makes 4 servings

nutrients per serving:

Calories 268
Calories from Fat 16%
Protein 12g
Carbohydrate 47g
Fiber 11g
Total Fat 5g
Saturated Fat 1g
Cholesterol 0mg
Sodium 541mg

Quinoa

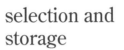

Pronounced KEEN-wah, this ancient grain that is becoming popular today is truly amazing. It provides a rich and balanced source of vital nutrients and more protein than any other grain.

benefits

Quinoa is a unique grain because its protein is considered complete, providing all of the essential amino acids, whereas other grains are missing the essential amino acid called lysine. It is also higher in unsaturated fats and lower in carbohydrates than most other grains. It's an excellent source of various minerals, including iron, magnesium, potassium, phosphorus and zinc, and it provides fiber, making it an all around healthy grain.

Phytonutrients called saponins in quinoa have anticancer and anti-inflammatory properties and may inhibit cholesterol absorption, too.

selection and storage

Quinoa is becoming more popular and is now available in many supermarkets near the rice and other grains. It is a tiny bead-shaped grain and may be available as red, black or ivory-colored. Quinoa should be stored in a sealed container in a cool, dry place or in the refrigerator. Quinoa is also available ground into flour and in several forms of pasta.

preparation and serving tips

Rinse quinoa in a fine-mesh sieve before cooking. Use one part quinoa to two parts water or broth. Bring to a simmer and reduce the heat to low. Cover and cook for 15 minutes or until quinoa is tender and the water is absorbed. Quinoa has a subtle, nutty flavor and can be substituted for other grains in almost any recipe. It works well as a change from rice, potatoes or pasta. It's even good at breakfast time as a hot cereal.

nutrients per serving:

Quinoa
½ cup cooked

Calories 111
Protein 4g
Total Fat 2g
Saturated Fat 0g
Cholesterol 0mg
Carbohydrate 20g
Dietary Fiber 2.5g
Sodium 6mg
Potassium 160mg
Iron 1.4mg
Zinc 1mg
Magnesium 59mg
Phosphorus 141mg
Folate 39mcg

breakfast quinoa

- ½ cup uncooked quinoa
- 1 cup water
- 1 tablespoon packed brown sugar
- 2 teaspoons maple syrup
- ½ teaspoon ground cinnamon
- ¼ cup golden raisins (optional)
- Raspberries and banana slices (optional)

1. Place quinoa in fine-mesh strainer; rinse well under cold running water. Transfer to small saucepan. Stir in water, brown sugar, maple syrup and cinnamon. Bring to a boil. Reduce heat; cover and simmer 15 minutes or until quinoa is tender and water is absorbed. Add raisins, if desired, during last 5 minutes of cooking.

2. Top quinoa with raspberries and bananas, if desired. *Makes 2 servings*

nutrients per serving:

Calories 233
Calories from Fat 12%
Protein 6g
Carbohydrate 47g
Fiber 4g
Total Fat 3g
Saturated Fat <1g
Cholesterol 0mg
Sodium 9mg

Raspberries

Raspberries are always a treat and a treasure. Tasting of summer, delicate raspberries almost melt in your mouth. It's hard to believe they're good for you, too.

nutrients per serving:

Raspberries
½ cup

Calories 32
Protein 1g
Total Fat 0g
Saturated Fat 0g
Cholesterol 0mg
Carbohydrate 7g
Dietary Fiber 4g
Sodium 0mg
Potassium 95mg
Calcium 15mg
Iron 0.4mg
Vitamin A 20 IU
Vitamin C 16mg
Folate 13mcg

benefits

Losing excess weight can lower your risk of heart disease, diabetes and other chronic ills. Treating yourself to luscious, low-calorie raspberries, with their jumbo fiber load, can help you do that without feeling hungry or deprived. With 8 grams of fiber per cup, raspberries fit well in a high-fiber diet, which is also associated with a lower risk of chronic diseases. Raspberries contain a cholesterol-lowering fiber called pectin, and the insoluble fiber in raspberry seeds helps prevent and treat constipation and other digestive woes. Raspberries also offer vitamin C and the phytochemical ellagic acid, both of which demonstrate anticancer properties.

selection and storage

Enjoy raspberries while they are in season during the summer. They are too fragile to travel or keep very well, and imported out-of-season berries are often disappointing as well as expensive. While most raspberries are red, there are also black, yellow and white varieties, each with its own slightly different flavor. Refrigerate unwashed berries and eat them within a day or two. Frozen unsweetened raspberries are also available.

preparation and serving tips

Rinse raspberries under cool water just before serving. Raspberries make an elegant addition to salads and desserts of all kinds. It's easy to make a raspberry sauce to pour over yogurt, angel food cake or ice cream. Just crush some berries with a bit of sugar and let them sit until juicy and saucy. If you have too many fresh raspberries for immediate use (Is that even possible?) lay them in a single layer on a baking sheet and freeze. Once frozen, transfer to a food storage bag.

poached spiced apples with raspberry sauce

1 package (12 ounces) frozen
    raspberries, thawed
¼ cup sugar
2 large Granny Smith or other tart
    apples, peeled and cored
1 cup apple cider
¼ to ½ teaspoon pumpkin pie spice
    Ice cream or frozen yogurt
    (optional)

1. Process raspberries and sugar in food processor or blender until smooth. Set aside. (Sauce can be chilled for several days at this point.)

2. Cut each apple into 8 wedges. Place apple wedges in medium saucepan with cider and pie spice. Bring to a boil over medium-high heat. Reduce heat; simmer 5 to 6 minutes or until apples are tender, turning occasionally. Using a slotted spoon, remove apples from poaching liquid. Spoon raspberry sauce over apples. Serve with ice cream, if desired. *Makes 4 servings*

nutrients per serving:

Calories 157
Calories from Fat <1%
Protein 3g
Carbohydrate 34g
Fiber 5g
Total Fat <1g
Saturated Fat 0g
Cholesterol 0mg
Sodium 1mg

Red Wine

Enjoying a glass of red wine with your evening meal can do more than make for a relaxing dinner. In moderation, red wine can also protect your heart and your health.

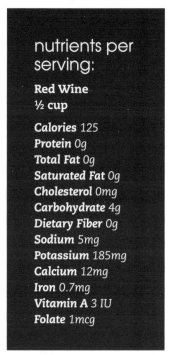

benefits

Studies have shown that moderate consumption of red wine—that's one to two 4-ounce glasses per day—is linked to a lower risk of heart disease. Antioxidants in the skin and seeds of red grapes used to make the wine may help prevent heart disease by lowering LDL ("bad") cholesterol and raising HDL ("good") cholesterol. An antioxidant called resveratrol may help reduce the risk of inflammation and blood clotting. Some studies even suggest red wine may help slow the aging process and offer protection from cancer and other age-related diseases. To gain any potential benefits, though, you have to pair that daily glass of wine with an overall healthy lifestyle.

selection and storage

There are many varieties of red wine, but the types associated with higher levels of antioxidants are the dry reds. Entire libraries have been written on choosing and tasting red wine. Fortunately, the best choice is the bottle that suits your palate, your budget and your menu. Store wine in a cool, dark place (55°F is ideal). Wines with corks need to be stored on their side to keep the cork moist and bottle properly sealed. An opened bottle of red wine can be recorked and stored in a dark place at room temperature for a day or two without losing quality.

preparation and serving tips

A glass of red wine can be enjoyed alone, but it achieves new dimensions when paired with an appropriate entrée or cheese. In cooking, wine enhances flavor and can even cut down the amount of fat you use.

Rye

Rye is a cereal grain most often ground into flour for breads. Their satisfying texture, earthy taste and good nutrition make pumpernickel and other hearty rye breads good additions to your breadbox.

benefits

Rye is particularly rich in water-absorbing insoluble fiber, which helps speed waste through the digestive tract. As a result, toxins spend less time in contact with the intestinal walls, potentially decreasing the risk of colon cancer. Rye also contains phytonutrients with anticancer activity equal to or higher than those from fruits and vegetables. In addition, rye's fiber helps reduce secretion of bile acids that can contribute to gallstone formation. And studies suggest that, compared to whole wheat bread, whole grain rye prompts less of an insulin response and appears better at satisfying hunger, lowering cholesterol and decreasing inflammation.

selection and storage

When choosing rye bread, darker is usually better.

Light rye is made from refined flour, which has lost much of the nutrition of the germ and bran. Most commercially processed rye bread also contains wheat flour. So check the ingredient list and look for whole grain rye (called "unbolted") as well as other whole grains. There are also many Scandinavian-style crisp breads or crackers that are made from whole grain rye.

preparation and serving tips

Rye breads are generally more compact and dense than wheat bread, so they work well for toasting and for sandwiches with hearty and moist fillings. Rye crisp breads go well with cheeses and smoked fish. Whole and cracked rye can be cooked and added to breakfast porridges, soups and stews.

nutrients per serving:

**Rye Bread
1 slice**

Calories 83
Protein 3g
Total Fat 1g
Saturated Fat 0g
Cholesterol 0mg
Carbohydrate 15g
Dietary Fiber 2g
Sodium 211mg
Potassium 53mg
Calcium 23mg
Iron 0.9mg
Thiamin 0.14mg
Riboflavin 0.1mg
Folate 35mcg

Salmon

The firm texture, full flavor and gorgeous color of salmon make it a favorite on the grill or in the oven. Get hooked on this healthy protein and skip the meat.

benefits

Salmon is a relatively fatty fish but, ironically, that's what makes it so good for you. Salmon's fat comes mostly in the form of omega-3 fish oils—polyunsaturated fats that play important roles in brain development, body functions and overall good health from infancy through old age. Omega-3s have also been shown to help prevent heart disease by reducing inflammation and lowering triglyceride (fat) levels in the blood. And they may help protect against Alzheimer's disease and depression. Because of these and other potential benefits, the government recommends we all eat fish twice a week.

selection and storage

Wild caught salmon is considered nutritionally superior to farm-raised, but it is also considerably more expensive and less available. Most Atlantic salmon is farmed; Alaskan salmon is usually wild caught. Whichever you choose, look for firm, fresh smelling fillets or steaks. (A fillet is from the side of the salmon, usually deboned and sometimes skinned; a steak is a vertical cut through the fish.) Store salmon in the coldest part of your refrigerator, usually towards the bottom in the back. Use it within a day or two. Salmon is also available frozen, canned, dried or smoked.

preparation and serving tips

Salmon is delicious grilled, baked, broiled, steamed or poached. It's naturally moist and flavorful and requires little seasoning beyond salt and pepper. Grilled or broiled, it pairs well with fresh fruit salsa. Combine leftover salmon with greens in a salad or add it to an omelet.

roast salmon with new potatoes and red onions

¼ cup reduced-sodium chicken broth
1 tablespoon olive or vegetable oil
1½ pounds small new potatoes, cut into halves
1 medium red onion, cut into ¼-inch-thick wedges
6 salmon fillets (4 ounces each)
¾ teaspoon salt (optional)
½ teaspoon black pepper
2 tablespoons chopped fresh tarragon

1. Preheat oven to 400°F. Spray large shallow roasting pan or jelly-roll pan with nonstick cooking spray.

2. Combine broth and oil in small bowl. Combine potatoes and half of broth mixture in prepared pan; toss to coat. Roast 20 minutes.

3. Add onion and remaining broth mixture to pan; toss to coat. Push vegetables to edges of pan; place salmon in center. Sprinkle salmon and vegetables with salt, if desired, and pepper. Roast 10 to 15 minutes or until center of salmon is opaque and vegetables are tender. Garnish with tarragon. *Makes 6 servings*

nutrients per serving:

Calories 276
Calories from Fat 16%
Protein 9g
Carbohydrate 22g
Fiber 3g
Total Fat 5g
Saturated Fat 1g
Cholesterol 18mg
Sodium 46mg

Sesame Seeds

These tiny seeds may often go unnoticed, but they add a nutty, slightly sweet taste and a delicate crunch— as well as a boost of nutrients—to many dishes.

benefits

Humble sesame seeds hide a host of beneficial nutrients. Their copper may help relieve rheumatoid arthritis and their iron is essential for producing oxygen-carrying red blood cells. Their magnesium supports the health of the lungs and blood vessels and works with the calcium and potassium in sesame seeds to keep blood pressure in a healthy range. The calcium helps maintain strong bones and teeth. Plus, sesame seeds contain cholesterol-lowering phytosterols and phytonutrients called lignans that have been shown to fight certain hormone-related cancers, including those of the breast and prostate.

selection and storage

Sesame seeds come in unhulled or hulled forms, toasted or untoasted. Hulled seeds, which are more common, are usually white or light yellow. Unhulled (whole) sesame seeds retain a thin, edible outer shell and can be red, brown or black. Store unhulled sesame seeds in an airtight container in a dry, cool, dark place; store hulled seeds in the refrigerator or freezer. Sesame oil, available plain or toasted, adds intense flavor to foods.

preparation and serving tips

Sesame seeds are the main ingredients in tahini (sesame seed paste) and the wonderful Middle Eastern sweet called halvah. Try adding sesame seeds to homemade breads, muffins or cookies. Sprinkle them over stir-fries or salads. Toasting sesame seeds intensifies their flavor. Combine toasted sesame seeds, rice vinegar, tamari and crushed garlic as a dressing for salads, vegetables or noodles.

nutrients per serving:

Sesame Seeds, unhulled
½ ounce

Calories 80
Protein 2g
Total Fat 7g
Saturated Fat 1g
Cholesterol 0mg
Carbohydrate 4g
Dietary Fiber 2g
Sodium 0mg
Potassium 65mg
Calcium 140mg
Iron 2.1mg
Magnesium 50mg
Copper 0.4mg
Phosphorus 90mg

benne wafers

6 tablespoons all-purpose flour
6 tablespoons whole wheat flour
¼ teaspoon salt
¼ teaspoon baking powder
½ cup sesame seeds
½ cup (1 stick) unsalted butter, softened
½ cup packed light brown sugar
1 egg
½ teaspoon vanilla

1. Preheat oven to 350°F. Line two baking sheets with parchment paper. Combine all-purpose flour, whole wheat flour, salt and baking powder in small bowl; set aside.

2. Spread sesame seeds on one baking sheet. Toast 5 minutes or until lightly browned. Transfer seeds to bowl to cool.

3. Beat butter and brown sugar in medium bowl with electric mixer at high speed until light and fluffy. Beat in egg and vanilla. Gradually beat in flour mixture. Add sesame seeds; beat until well blended.

4. Drop dough by rounded teaspoonfuls 2 inches apart onto prepared baking sheets. Flatten slightly with fork. Bake 10 minutes or until lightly browned. Cool on baking sheets 5 minutes; remove to wire rack to cool completely.   *Makes about 48 wafers*

nutrients per serving:

Calories 43
Calories from Fat 58%
Protein <1g

Carbohydrate 4g
Fiber <1g
Total Fat 3g
Saturated Fat 1g
Cholesterol 9mg
Sodium 18mg

Shellfish

This seafood category includes any water-dwelling creature with its skeleton on the outside—oysters, clams, mussels, lobster, shrimp, crab, scallops and others.

benefits

Shellfish supply omega-3s—polyunsaturated fats associated with a lower risk of heart disease, certain cancers and age-related eye diseases that are among the leading causes of blindness, such as retinopathy and macular degeneration. Research also suggests that omega-3s are important to cognitive function and may help lower elevated blood pressure and reduce joint inflammation in arthritis. Although shellfish are rich in omega-3s, they are low in total fat compared to most complete protein sources. And they're very low in cholesterol-raising saturated fat. Shellfish also contain more heart-protective vitamin B_{12} and fewer calories, ounce for ounce, than other sources of animal protein.

nutrients per serving:

Shrimp
3 ounces cooked

Calories 101
Protein 19g
Total Fat 2g
Saturated Fat 0g
Cholesterol 179mg
Carbohydrate 1g
Dietary Fiber 0g
Sodium 805mg
Potassium 145mg
Calcium 77mg
Iron 0.3mg
Magnesium 31mg
Copper 0.2mg
Vitamin B_{12} 1.4mcg

selection and storage

Always buy fresh shellfish from a trusted source with a large turnover. With the exception of shrimp, scallops and crabmeat, fresh shellfish should be kept alive until ready to cook. Lobsters should be active, not sluggish. Oysters, mussels and clams should close their shells when tapped. Avoid any with cracked shells. Fresh shellfish should be eaten within one or two days. Frozen shellfish is often a good bet since it is flash frozen at the time of harvest.

preparation and serving tips

Frozen shellfish should be thawed in the refrigerator before cooking. Always keep shellfish cold, treat it with care and discard any that looks or smells off. Don't overcook shellfish or it will be rubbery and tough. Bivalves should be steamed just until they open. Discard any unopened shells. To devein shrimp (not absolutely necessary), make a shallow cut along the rounded side and use the tip of a knife or your fingers to remove the black stringlike vein.

crab and pasta salad in cantaloupe

1½ cups uncooked rotini pasta
1 cup seedless green grapes
½ cup chopped celery
½ cup fresh pineapple chunks
1 small red onion, coarsely chopped
6 ounces canned, fresh or frozen
    crabmeat, drained
½ cup plain nonfat yogurt
¼ cup mayonnaise
2 teaspoons grated lemon peel
2 tablespoons lemon juice
2 tablespoons honey
1 teaspoon Dijon mustard
2 small cantaloupes

1. Cook pasta according to package directions. Rinse under cold water; drain and set aside.

2. Combine grapes, celery, pineapple, onion and crabmeat in large bowl. Combine yogurt, mayonnaise, lemon peel, lemon juice, honey and mustard in small bowl. Add yogurt mixture and pasta to crabmeat mixture. Stir to coat evenly. Cover and refrigerate.

3. Just before serving, cut cantaloupes in half. Remove and discard seeds. Remove some cantaloupe with spoon, leaving a shell about ¾ inch thick. Fill cantaloupes with salad.

Makes 4 servings

nutrients per serving:

Calories 331
Calories from Fat 17%
Protein 14g

Carbohydrate 56g
Fiber 1g
Total Fat 6g
Saturated Fat 1g
Cholesterol 42mg
Sodium 463mg

Spinach

We all know that leafy greens are good for us because they lower the risk of all sorts of diseases. Spinach just may be the one that's best tasting, simplest to prepare and easiest to love.

health benefits

Spinach has an amazingly rich mix of essential nutrients with antioxidant functions, including vitamins C, E and A and the minerals manganese, selenium and zinc. Spinach also provides more than a dozen antioxidant and anti-inflammatory phytonutrients. This makes spinach helpful in fighting high blood pressure, hardening of the arteries, heart disease and stroke; various cancers, including those of the stomach, skin, prostate and breast; and eye diseases such as cataracts and macular degeneration. Spinach also contributes iron and folic acid for healthy red blood cells.

selection and storage

Choose spinach with crisp, dark green leaves. There are many varieties, some with crinkled, arrow-shaped leaves and others with leaves that are flat and round. Unwashed spinach stored in a loose plastic bag in the refrigerator will keep for three to four days.

To wash fresh spinach, fill the sink or a large container with cold water and swish the leaves around. Repeat with fresh water until no more dirt is deposited. Frozen or prewashed fresh spinach is also available.

preparation and serving tips

Alone or mixed with other vegetables, raw spinach makes a wonderful salad. Chopped raw spinach can be added to many different dishes to boost nutrients, such as soups, pasta sauces, casseroles and meat loaves. To serve cooked spinach as a side, simmer the leaves in a small amount of water just until they begin to wilt, about 5 minutes. Top with lemon juice, balsamic vinegar, sautéed garlic, soy sauce or a dash of nutmeg.

wilted spinach salad with white beans & olives

- 2 thick slices bacon, diced
- ½ cup chopped onion
- 1 can (about 15 ounces) navy beans, rinsed and drained
- ½ cup halved pitted kalamata or black olives
- 1 package (9 ounces) baby spinach
- 1 cup cherry tomatoes (cut in half if large)
- 1½ tablespoons balsamic vinegar
- Black pepper (optional)

1. Cook bacon in Dutch oven or large saucepan over medium heat 2 minutes. Add onion; cook, stirring occasionally, 5 to 6 minutes or until bacon is crisp and onion is tender. Stir in beans and olives; heat through.

2. Add spinach, tomatoes and vinegar; cover and cook 1 minute or until spinach is slightly wilted. Toss lightly. Season with pepper, if desired.

Makes 4 servings

nutrients per serving:

Calories 230
Calories from Fat 20%
Protein 13g
Carbohydrate 35g
Fiber 14g
Total Fat 5g
Saturated Fat 1g
Cholesterol 5mg
Sodium 324mg

Strawberries

Luscious strawberries are the only fruit with seeds on the outside rather than on the inside. Perfectly ripe strawberries need no extra sweeteners, toppings or accompaniments.

benefits

As with all berries, strawberries are a fabulous fiber find, with their little seeds providing insoluble fiber that keeps you regular and helps fend off digestive system woes, including hemorrhoids and constipation. These popular berries are also a super source of disease-fighting, immunity-boosting vitamin C—an even better source than oranges and grapefruit. Strawberries pack plenty of potassium, an essential mineral that helps the body maintain a healthy blood pressure and so may help prevent strokes. Strawberries also contain ellagic acid, a phytonutrient with cancer-fighting and anti-inflammatory power.

selection and storage

Look for plump, ruby red, evenly colored strawberries with fresh, green, leafy tops. Avoid soft, mushy or moldy berries. Large size does not mean extra flavor; in fact, smaller berries tend to be sweeter. Avoid strawberries in juice-stained containers or those packed tightly with plastic wrap. Strawberries spoil quickly, so buy within a day or two of serving. Refrigerate strawberries unwashed and loosely covered.

preparation and serving tips

Strawberries can perk up cereal, add pizzazz to salad or make pudding or yogurt a real treat. If strawberries become overripe, purée and add them to smoothies or fruit drinks, or drizzle the purée over angel food cake or low-fat ice cream. To bring out strawberries' sweetness, add a splash of balsamic vinegar.

nutrients per serving:

Strawberries
1 cup halves

Calories 49
Protein 1g
Total Fat 0g
Saturated Fat 0g
Cholesterol 0mg
Carbohydrate 12g
Dietary Fiber 3g
Sodium 0mg
Potassium 235mg
Calcium 24mg
Iron 0.6mg
Vitamin A 18 IU
Vitamin C 89mg
Folate 36mcg

summer strawberry orange cups

- 2 cups stemmed fresh strawberries, divided
- 1 packet (¼ ounce) unflavored gelatin
- 2 tablespoons cold water
- 2 tablespoons boiling water
- 1½ cups reduced-fat (2%) milk
- ½ cup frozen orange juice concentrate
- 1 teaspoon vanilla

1. Thinly slice 1 cup strawberries; place in bottom of six 8-ounce dessert bowls or custard cups.

2. Combine gelatin and cold water in small bowl; let stand 5 minutes. Add boiling water; stir until completely dissolved.

3. Combine milk, orange juice concentrate and vanilla in medium bowl; mix well. Let stand at room temperature 20 minutes. Stir in gelatin mixture until well blended. Pour evenly over sliced strawberries in bowls. Refrigerate 2 hours or until completely set.

4. Slice remaining 1 cup strawberries; arrange on top of each dessert.

Makes 6 servings

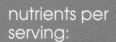

nutrients per serving:

Calories 268
Calories from Fat 16%
Protein 12g

Carbohydrate 47g
Fiber 11g
Total Fat 5g
Saturated Fat 1g
Cholesterol 0mg
Sodium 541mg

Sunflower Seeds

Sunflower seeds are a tasty gift from the tall, beautiful sunflower. The kernels within the black-and-white-striped shells make a wonderful, nutritious snack.

benefits

Sunflower seeds contain heart-healthy polyunsaturated fat as well as natural cholesterol-lowering phytosterols. They're an excellent source of vitamin E, the body's primary fat-soluble antioxidant, which has anti-inflammatory effects that help protect the heart and reduce the risk of cancer. They're also a good source of magnesium, which helps lower high blood pressure, prevent migraine headaches, maintain healthy bones and support energy production. And the selenium in sunflower seeds has been shown to help prevent or slow the growth of cancer cells.

selection and storage

Sunflower seeds are sold shelled or unshelled, salted or unsalted and dry or oil roasted. For less fat and sodium, choose dry roasted, unsalted seeds. When purchasing whole seeds, look for firm shells that are not cracked or dirty. When purchasing shelled seeds, avoid those that appear yellowish in color. Sunflower seeds have a high fat content and are prone to rancidity. Store them in an airtight container in the refrigerator or in the freezer to extend their shelf life.

preparation and serving tips

Besides enjoying them as a snack, use sunflower seeds to lend crunch and flavor to many different foods. Try adding them to green salads, tuna or chicken salads or stir-fries. Sprinkle them on hot or cold cereals or add them to pancakes, muffins or cookies. Use them in a recipe to make your own energy bars or as a topping for homemade breads or rolls.

nutrients per serving:

**Sunflower Seeds, kernels, dry roasted without salt
½ ounce**

Calories 82
Protein 3g
Total Fat 7g
Saturated Fat 0.5g
Cholesterol 0mg
Carbohydrate 3g
Dietary Fiber 1.5g
Sodium 0mg
Potassium 120mg
Calcium 10mg
Iron 0.5mg
Vitamin A 1 IU

sunny seed bran waffles

    2 egg whites
    1 tablespoon dark brown sugar
    1 tablespoon canola or vegetable oil
    1 cup fat-free (skim) milk
    ⅔ cup unprocessed wheat bran
    ⅔ cup quick oats
  1½ teaspoons baking powder
    ¼ teaspoon salt
    3 tablespoons sunflower seeds, toasted*
    1 cup apple butter (optional)

*To toast sunflower seeds, spread in small skillet. Shake
skillet over medium heat 2 minutes or until seeds begin
to pop and turn golden.

1. Beat egg whites in medium bowl with
electric mixer at medium-high speed until
soft peaks form; set aside. Mix brown sugar
and oil in small bowl. Stir in milk; mix well.
Combine bran, oats, baking powder and salt
in large bowl; mix well. Stir milk mixture into
bran mixture. Add sunflower seeds; stir just
until moistened. *Do not overmix.* Gently fold in
beaten egg whites.

2. Spray nonstick waffle iron lightly
with cooking spray; heat according to
manufacturer's directions. Stir batter; spoon
½ cup batter into waffle iron for each waffle.
Cook until steam stops escaping from around
edges and waffle is golden brown. Serve
waffles with apple butter, if desired.

Makes 4 waffles

Note: It is essential to use a nonstick waffle
iron because of the low fat content of these
waffles.

nutrients per serving:

Calories 190
Calories from Fat 38%
Protein 9g
Carbohydrate 24g
Fiber 6g
Total Fat 8g
Saturated Fat 1g
Cholesterol 1mg
Sodium 359mg

Sweet Potatoes

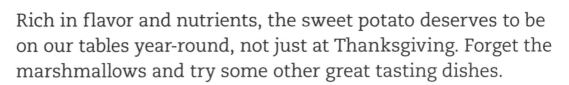

Rich in flavor and nutrients, the sweet potato deserves to be on our tables year-round, not just at Thanksgiving. Forget the marshmallows and try some other great tasting dishes.

nutrients per serving:

Sweet Potato
½ cup cooked

Calories 90
Protein 2g
Total Fat 0g
Saturated Fat 0g
Cholesterol 0mg
Carbohydrate 21g
Dietary Fiber 3.5g
Sodium 35mg
Potassium 475mg
Calcium 38mg
Iron 0.7mg
Vitamin A 19,218 IU
Vitamin C 20mg
Folate 6mcg

benefits

This starchy vegetable has bulk to keep you satisfied and an impressive nutrient roster. Its fiber alone is enough to make a sweet potato worth eating, since a diet rich in fiber is associated with a lower risk of all sorts of health problems, from constipation to heart attacks. It also provides an enormous helping of vitamin A in the form of antioxidant beta-carotene, making it a top-flight weapon for fighting chronic diseases such as cancer and heart disease and inflammation-related conditions such as asthma and rheumatoid arthritis. The sweet potato is also rich in infection-fighting, immunity-boosting vitamin C and in potassium, that boon to healthy blood pressure.

selection and storage

Though often called a yam, the sweet potato is a different vegetable and is not related to the common potato either. Look for firm sweet potatoes that are small to medium in size with smooth, unbruised skin. Though sweet potatoes look hardy, they're actually quite fragile and spoil easily. Store them in a dry, dark, well-ventilated cupboard, not the refrigerator. Use them within a week.

preparation and serving tips

Boil, bake or microwave unpeeled sweet potatoes. Leaving the peel intact prevents excessive loss of nutrients and locks in natural sweetness. Try sweet potatoes mashed, roasted, in a soufflé or in traditional southern sweet potato pie. Use sweet potato to add moistness and flavor to quick breads or muffins.

sweet potato pie

1 large or 2 medium sweet potatoes
   (1½ to 2 pounds), peeled and
   diced
1½ to 2 cups water
½ cup sugar
¼ cup (½ stick) margarine
¼ cup low-fat buttermilk
1 egg
1 egg white
½ teaspoon vanilla
1 unbaked reduced-fat deep-dish
   pie crust

1. Place potatoes in large saucepan; cover with water. Bring to a boil; cook 15 to 20 minutes or until fork-tender.

2. Preheat oven to 375°F.

3. Beat potatoes in large bowl with electric mixer at medium speed until smooth. Add sugar and margarine; beat until well blended. Combine buttermilk, egg, egg white and vanilla in small bowl; mix well. Add to potatoes; beat until well blended.

4. Pour mixture into unbaked pie crust. Bake 1 hour or until center is set. Cool on wire rack.

Makes 10 servings

nutrients per serving:

Calories 184
Calories from Fat 49%
Protein 2g

Carbohydrate 21g
Fiber <1g
Total Fat 10g
Saturated Fat 1g
Cholesterol 25mg
Sodium 128mg

Tea

Tea has started revolutions, created traditions and been celebrated as an elixir for thousands of years. Whether you prefer green or black, hot or iced, tea can lift your mood and improve your health.

nutrients per serving:

Tea, black
1 cup brewed

Calories 2
Protein 0g
Total Fat 0g
Saturated Fat 0g
Cholesterol 0mg
Carbohydrate 1g
Dietary Fiber 0g
Sodium 5mg
Potassium 90mg
Iron 0.1mg
Folate 12mcg

benefits

Tea is rich in antioxidants called flavonoids. These compounds help prevent oxidation of cholesterol, making it less likely to stick to artery walls. They also help ward off heart attack and stroke by working to prevent blood clots and damage to blood vessels. In addition, tea appears to offer some protection against various cancers by interfering with the ability of cancerous cells to replicate. And research suggests tea may help suppress the growth of infection-causing bacteria. These benefits are associated with drinking 2 to 3 cups per day.

selection and storage

All teas (except herbal) come from the *Camellia sinensis* plant. The differences in color and flavor depend primarily on how the leaves are processed. Green tea is from leaves that are dried soon after harvesting. Black and oolong teas are partially dried, crushed and fermented to varying degrees. White tea comes from buds and new leaves picked in the early spring. The highest quality teas are sold in the form of loose leaves, but many varieties are also available in bags. Store tea in a cool, dry, dark cupboard, not the refrigerator. Instant tea, bottled tea and herbal tea do not offer the same health benefits.

preparation and serving tips

White and green teas should be brewed at a lower temperature (140°F to 180°F) than oolong and black teas (195°F). Loose tea leaves can be brewed in a pot or tea ball. For best flavor, steep most green teas for 1 to 3 minutes; black teas for 3 to 5 minutes. Adding honey, sugar, lemon or milk adds calories and can also easily overpower delicate flavors.

thai coconut iced tea

- **2 bags jasmine tea or other black tea**
- **2 cups boiling water**
- **1 cup unsweetened canned coconut milk**
- **2 packets sugar substitute**

1. Brew 2 cups jasmine tea with boiling water according to package directions; cool to room temperature.

2. Combine ½ cup coconut milk and 1 packet sugar substitute in each of two glasses; stir until dissolved. Add ice; carefully pour half of tea into each glass. Serve immediately.   *Makes 2 servings*

Tip: For a more dramatic presentation, gently pour tea over the back of a spoon held close to the surface of the coconut milk in each glass. The tea will pool in a layer on the coconut milk before blending.

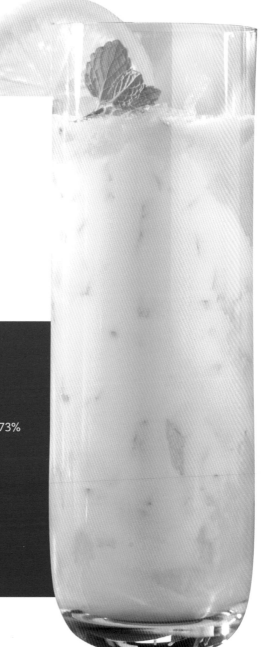

nutrients per serving:

Calories 74
Calories from Fat 73%
Protein 0g
Carbohydrate 5g
Fiber 0g
Total Fat 6g
Saturated Fat 4g
Cholesterol 0mg
Sodium 44mg

Tofu

You can bake it, stir-fry it, grill it, poach it or eat it as is. Tofu can be turned into creamy sauces or take the place of meat. The mild, clean taste works with whatever flavors you favor, from hot and spicy to rich and hearty.

nutrients per serving:

Tofu, regular
½ cup

Calories 94
Protein 10g
Total Fat 6g
Saturated Fat 1g
Cholesterol 0mg
Carbohydrate 2g
Dietary Fiber 0.5g
Sodium 10mg
Potassium 150mg
Calcium 434mg
Iron 6.7mg
Vitamin A 105 IU
Folate 19mcg

benefits

Tofu, like meat, provides complete protein, which contains all the amino acids we need from food, and also supplies beneficial amounts of iron, key to getting oxygen to our cells. Compared to meat, however, tofu has fewer calories and no cholesterol. Tofu, like other soy foods containing soy isoflavones and phytonutrients, has been linked to less risk of heart disease and some cancers and relief of menopausal symptoms. And tofu processed with calcium sulphate can be high in calcium, a mineral we all need for strong bones.

selection and storage

Regular tofu comes in soft, firm or extra-firm textures. It is packed in water and found in the refrigerated section. Once opened, regular tofu will keep in the refrigerator up to four days. (Water should be drained and replaced daily.) Silken tofu, which has a more custardlike texture, is found in unrefrigerated, aseptically sealed packages and is a good choice for soups or sauces.

preparation and serving tips

Recipes sometimes call for pressing tofu to remove some of the water and make it firmer. To press tofu, place it on a cutting board lined with paper towels. Cover with more paper towels and put a flat, heavy object on top for about 15 minutes. Tofu takes extremely well to marinades and sauces since it absorbs flavors easily. Crumbled tofu can be a substitute for cheese, and soft tofu is delicious blended in a smoothie or salad dressing.

zesty vegetarian chili

- 1 tablespoon canola or vegetable oil
- 1 large red bell pepper, coarsely chopped
- 2 medium zucchini or yellow squash (or 1 of each), cut into ½-inch chunks
- 4 cloves garlic, minced
- 1 can (about 14 ounces) fire-roasted diced tomatoes
- ¾ cup chunky salsa
- 2 teaspoons chili powder
- 1 teaspoon dried oregano
- 1 can (about 15 ounces) no-salt-added red kidney beans, rinsed and drained
- 10 ounces extra-firm tofu, well drained and cut into ½-inch cubes
  Chopped fresh cilantro (optional)

1. Heat oil in large saucepan over medium heat. Add bell pepper; cook and stir 4 minutes. Add zucchini and garlic; cook and stir 3 minutes.

2. Stir in tomatoes, salsa, chili powder and oregano; bring to a boil over high heat. Reduce heat to low; simmer 15 minutes or until vegetables are tender.

3. Stir beans and tofu into chili. Simmer 2 minutes or until heated through. Garnish with cilantro. *Makes 4 servings*

nutrients per serving:

Calories 231
Calories from Fat 31%
Protein 15g
Carbohydrate 28g
Fiber 8g
Total Fat 8g
Saturated Fat 1g
Cholesterol 0mg
Sodium 432mg

Tomatoes

Raw or cooked, in sauces or salads, tomatoes add color, flavor and texture to every kind of dish. This is one sweet super food that's easy to enjoy every day.

benefits

Tomatoes are low in calories and fat free, so they naturally lend themselves to healthy cooking. They are also an important source of some key disease fighters. The vitamin C in tomatoes is an antioxidant that supports healthy immune function. Their beta-carotene and other carotenoids are powerful weapons against heart disease, cancer and other chronic ills. And the antioxidant lycopene, which makes tomatoes red, may help reduce the risk of cardiovascular disease and prostate cancer. Tomatoes also offer a good dose of potassium, which works to maintain healthy blood pressure.

selection and storage

Tomatoes come in a range of cheery colors—bright red, yellow, striped with yellow or green, even almost black. Choose the size that works for the recipe you're making. You can pick a lovely round slicer, tiny grape tomatoes or anything in between. Real tomato taste comes only in season. Fortunately, canned tomatoes are ready to use any time and are nutritionally close to fresh. The best way to choose fresh tomatoes is by scent; if they have no aroma, they won't have any taste either. Don't store fresh tomatoes in the refrigerator as it ruins their flavor and texture.

preparation and serving tips

Try different colors and varieties of tomatoes in salads for taste and eye appeal. Roasting tomatoes concentrates their flavor. Halve or quarter tomatoes and place in a single layer on a baking sheet lined with parchment. Sprinkle with salt, pepper and herbs and drizzle with olive oil. Roast at 300°F for about 45 minutes or until they shrink and become dry.

nutrients per serving:

**Tomato
1 medium**

Calories 80
Protein 2g
Total Fat 7g
Saturated Fat 1g
Cholesterol 0mg
Carbohydrate 4g
Dietary Fiber 2g
Sodium 0mg
Potassium 65mg
Calcium 140mg
Iron 2.1mg
Magnesium 50mg
Copper 0.4mg
Phosphorus 90mg

flank steak with italian salsa

- 2 tablespoons olive oil
- 2 teaspoons balsamic vinegar
- 1½ pounds lean flank steak
- 1 tablespoon minced garlic
- ¾ teaspoon salt, divided
- ¾ teaspoon black pepper, divided
- 1 cup diced plum tomatoes
- ⅓ cup chopped pitted kalamata olives
- 2 tablespoons chopped fresh basil

1. Whisk oil and vinegar in medium glass bowl. Place steak in shallow dish; spread with garlic. Sprinkle with ½ teaspoon salt and ½ teaspoon pepper. Spoon 2 tablespoons oil mixture over steak. Cover; marinate in refrigerator at least 20 minutes or up to 2 hours.

2. Prepare grill for direct cooking. For salsa, combine tomatoes, olives, basil, remaining ¼ teaspoon salt and ¼ teaspoon pepper with remaining 2 teaspoons oil mixture in medium bowl; mix well. Set aside.

3. Drain steak; discard marinade. Let garlic remain on steak. Grill steak over medium-high heat 5 to 6 minutes per side for medium rare.

4. Transfer steak to carving board. Tent with foil; let stand 5 minutes. Cut across grain into thin slices. Serve with tomato salsa.

Makes 6 servings

nutrients per serving:

Calories 191
Calories from Fat 54%
Protein 18g

Carbohydrate 4g
Fiber 1g
Total Fat 11g
Saturated Fat 3g
Cholesterol 35mg
Sodium 407mg

Turnips

Turnips are one of the prettiest and most underappreciated root vegetables. Use them in place of potatoes for fewer calories, and enjoy the nutritious greens as well.

benefits

Turnips are a source of soluble fiber, which helps soak up cholesterol and prevent large fluctuations in blood sugar, as well as vitamin C, a potent antioxidant that helps protect the heart and promote a healthy immune system. Turnips contain lysine, an amino acid useful in preventing and treating cold sores. In addition, the potassium and calcium in turnips work to keep blood pressure in a normal range. Turnip greens are even more nutrient dense, providing twice the vitamin C and even more calcium and potassium. They also add disease-fighting beta-carotene to the mix.

selection and storage

Turnips are available year-round, but the best ones come to market in the fall. Baby turnips are the most tender and sweet and can be eaten whole, greens and all. The most common turnip variety is white with purple markings around the top. Yellow turnips are also called rutabagas. Japanese turnips are small and pure white; they look and taste similar to a radish. Look for turnips with smooth, blemish-free skin. Store them in the refrigerator crisper and use within a week or so. Remove and store the leaves separately.

preparation and serving tips

To prepare turnips, first remove the leaf and root ends. Larger turnips should be peeled, but smaller turnips can be cooked without peeling. Baby turnips can be eaten raw in salads. Like other root vegetables, turnips are delicious roasted or baked. Mash some turnips along with potatoes for a more interesting side dish. Turnip greens have a sharp, peppery flavor that mellows after cooking.

nutrients per serving:

Turnips
½ cup cooked

Calories 17
Protein 1g
Total Fat 0g
Saturated Fat 0g
Cholesterol 0mg
Carbohydrate 4g
Dietary Fiber 1.5g
Sodium 10mg
Potassium 140mg
Calcium 26mg
Iron 0.1mg
Vitamin C 9mg
Folate 7mcg

curried chicken & winter vegetable stew

Nonstick cooking spray
1 pound boneless skinless chicken breasts, cut into ½-inch cubes
1 tablespoon curry powder
3½ cups fat-free reduced-sodium chicken broth
1 can (about 14 ounces) no-salt-added diced tomatoes
2 medium turnips, cut into 1-inch pieces
2 medium carrots, cut into 1-inch pieces
1 medium onion, chopped
¼ cup no-salt-added tomato paste
½ cup raisins (optional)

1. Spray large saucepan with cooking spray; heat over medium heat. Cook chicken 5 minutes or until lightly browned. Add curry powder; cook and stir 1 minute.

2. Stir in broth, tomatoes, turnips, carrots, onion, tomato paste and raisins, if desired. Bring to a boil. Reduce heat; simmer, covered, stirring occasionally, 15 minutes or until vegetables are tender.   *Makes 6 servings*

Serving Suggestion: Serve with couscous or brown rice.

nutrients per serving:

Calories 140
Calories from Fat 13%
Protein 18g
Carbohydrate 12g
Fiber 3g
Total Fat 2g
Saturated Fat 0g
Cholesterol 50mg
Sodium 410mg

Walnuts

Walnuts add flavor, crunch and good nutrition to any meal or snack. No wonder they were called the food of the gods in ancient Rome.

benefits

Compared to other nuts, walnuts provide the most omega-3 fats, which research suggests can help protect the heart and blood vessels from disease; promote better brain function; and fight the inflammation associated with diseases such as arthritis, asthma and psoriasis. Other common nuts also trail far behind walnuts in the amount and quality of their antioxidants, which boost disease resistance and protect the body's cells from damage. Plus, walnuts supply protein and fiber to help satisfy hunger, lower blood cholesterol and keep blood sugar in check. They do also pack calories, however, so enjoy them in moderation.

selection and storage

Walnuts are most often available shelled but can also be purchased in the shell. Shells should be free of cracks or holes. Shelled walnuts come in halves, pieces, chopped or ground. They should be dry and crisp, not limp or shriveled. Store shelled nuts in an airtight container in the refrigerator for up to six months. In the shell, walnuts will keep for four to six months in a cool, dry place.

preparation and serving tips

Walnuts are tasty on their own or chopped and added to cookies, cereals, salads, vegetable dishes, muffins, quick breads, pancakes and more. Toasting them brings out their flavor. Simply arrange walnuts in a single layer on a baking sheet and bake at 350°F for 5 to 7 minutes or until fragrant and lightly browned. Try adding finely chopped walnuts to the breading for chicken or fish.

orange-walnut bread

- 1¾ cups all-purpose flour
- ½ cup plus 1 tablespoon sugar, divided
- 1 tablespoon grated orange peel
- 1½ teaspoons baking powder
- ¼ teaspoon baking soda
- ¼ teaspoon salt
- ¾ cup low-fat buttermilk
- ⅓ cup plus 2 tablespoons orange juice, divided
- ¼ cup vegetable oil
- 1 egg, lightly beaten
- ½ cup chopped walnuts

1. Preheat oven to 350°F. Grease 8×4-inch loaf pan. Combine flour, ½ cup sugar, orange peel, baking powder, baking soda and salt in medium bowl.

2. Stir together buttermilk, ⅓ cup orange juice, oil and egg in small bowl until blended. Add buttermilk mixture to flour mixture; stir just until moistened. Fold in walnuts.

3. Spoon batter into prepared pan. Bake 50 to 55 minutes or until toothpick inserted into center comes out clean.

4. Whisk remaining 2 tablespoons orange juice and 1 tablespoon sugar in small bowl or cup until sugar dissolves. Brush glaze over warm bread. Cool in pan 10 minutes. Remove to wire rack; cool completely. Wrap in plastic wrap. Store overnight before slicing.

Makes 12 servings

nutrients per serving:

Calories 191
Calories from Fat 40%
Protein 4g
Carbohydrate 26g
Fiber 1g
Total Fat 9g
Saturated Fat 1g
Cholesterol 18mg
Sodium 158mg

Watercress

These delicate green leaves have a surprisingly robust, peppery flavor. A member of the cruciferous vegetable family, watercress is among the more nutritious salad greens.

benefits

Like other cruciferous vegetables, watercress is rich in antioxidant compounds, including lutein and beta-carotene, which help to protect the eyes from damage and combat the deleterious effects of free radicals that can lead to the development and growth of cancerous cells. Watercress has also been found to contain phytonutrients that aid detoxification and help protect against lung cancer. And the vitamin C and other antioxidants in watercress work together to reduce the risk of heart disease and cancer, boost the activity of the immune system and keep the gums healthy. In addition, the calcium and potassium in watercress help to normalize blood pressure.

selection and storage

Watercress is available year-round, usually sold in small bunches. Look for crisp leaves with deep, vibrant color. There should be no signs of yellowing or wilting. Stored in the refrigerator in a plastic bag or, better yet, with the stems in a glass of water and the leaves covered with a plastic bag, it should last up to five days.

preparation and serving tips

Rinse watercress well and shake or spin dry right before using. Use watercress in salads and to line plates. It makes a nice change from lettuce in a sandwich. The peppery flavor of watercress works well with citrus or sweet fruits, including grapefruit, orange, melon or strawberry. The smooth richness of avocado is also a nice contrast to watercress's crisp crunch and slight bitterness.

nutrients per serving:

Watercress
1 cup

Calories 4
Protein 1g
Total Fat 0g
Saturated Fat 0g
Cholesterol 0mg
Carbohydrate <1g
Dietary Fiber <1g
Sodium 15mg
Potassium 110mg
Calcium 41mg
Iron 0.1mg
Vitamin A 1,085 IU
Vitamin C 15mg
Folate 3mcg

2 tablespoons lime juice
2 tablespoons red wine vinegar
1 teaspoon sugar
1 bunch watercress, trimmed
1 avocado, sliced
2 cups cantaloupe balls

1. Combine 1 cup strawberries, oil, lime juice, vinegar and sugar in food processor; process until smooth. Strain mixture through fine-mesh sieve; discard solids.

2. Arrange watercress on plates; top with avocado, cantaloupe and remaining 1 cup strawberries. Drizzle with vinaigrette.

Makes 4 servings

nutrients per serving:

Calories 160
Calories from Fat 68%
Protein 3g
Carbohydrate 14g
Fiber 4g
Total Fat 12g
Saturated Fat 2g
Cholesterol 0mg
Sodium 40mg

Watermelon

It just wouldn't be a picnic or a barbecue without a slice of ice-cold, sweet, juicy watermelon for dessert. The bonus is that while watermelon satisfies your thirst and sweet tooth, it's doing your body good.

nutrients per serving:

Watermelon
1 cup

Calories 46
Protein 1g
Total Fat 0g
Saturated Fat 0g
Cholesterol 0mg
Carbohydrate 11g
Dietary Fiber 0.5g
Sodium 0mg
Potassium 170mg
Calcium 11mg
Iron 0.4mg
Vitamin A 865 IU
Vitamin C 12mg
Folate 5mcg

benefits

Watermelon is unique among melons in that it is a valuable source of the phytonutrient lycopene, which has been shown to reduce the risk of prostate, breast and colon cancers. Watermelon is also a decent source of potassium, which helps to keep blood pressure in a healthy range and may reduce the risk of developing kidney stones and, possibly, age-related bone loss. Watermelon's abundant supplies of disease-fighting vitamin C and vitamin A (as beta-carotene) participate in the body's defenses against heart disease, cancer and other chronic conditions.

selection and storage

There are many varieties of watermelon, including seedless. Look for watermelons that are evenly shaped with no bruises, cracks or soft spots. Select ones that are heavy for their size and sound hollow when tapped. If you're buying precut pieces, the surface should look moist and juicy. A whole watermelon keeps in the refrigerator a week or more. Once sliced, wrap the pieces tightly in plastic wrap and refrigerate for only a few days.

preparation and serving tips

Rinse watermelon well before cutting. The flesh can be cubed, sliced or scooped into balls. Watermelon tastes best when it's served icy cold. It can be used to make a cold melon soup or paired with a salty cheese such as feta for a refreshing snack. A hollowed-out watermelon rind makes a wonderful serving bowl for fruit salad.

Wheat Berries

Wheat berries are whole, unprocessed kernels of wheat. Their chewy bite and subtle, nutty flavor make them a more nutritious substitute for other grains or starches.

benefits

Because they are unrefined, wheat berries retain all their natural nutrients plus a hefty amount of insoluble fiber to keep you regular. They're a good source of magnesium, which supports strong immune function, sturdy bones and a steady heart rhythm. Magnesium also works with potassium to maintain normal blood pressure and may help prevent type 2 diabetes. Wheat berries also provide decent amounts of iron, that essential oxygen carrier, and the antioxidant mineral selenium, which helps regulate thyroid activity.

selection and storage

Wheat berries are often available prepackaged in the natural foods section or in the bulk grain section of supermarkets. Most wheat berries are hard red winter wheat, which is higher in protein than soft spring wheat. In addition to being cooked, wheat berries can be sprouted or ground into whole wheat flour. Store wheat berries in an airtight container in a dry, cool place for up to a year.

preparation and serving tips

Before cooking, rinse wheat berries under cool water. Place them in a large saucepan and cover with water. (Cooked, they will double in volume, so plan accordingly.) Bring to a boil, reduce heat, cover and simmer for 45 minutes to 1 hour or until they soften to a firm but chewy consistency. Drain and serve warm or refrigerate to serve cold. Add cooked wheat berries to soups, salads and side dishes. Or serve them as a breakfast cereal with fruit and milk.

nutrients per serving:

Wheat Berries
½ cup cooked

Calories 158
Protein 7g
Total Fat 0.5g
Saturated Fat 0g
Cholesterol 0mg
Carbohydrate 33g
Dietary Fiber 6g
Sodium 0mg
Potassium 163mg
Calcium 12mg
Iron 1.7mg
Magnesium 60mg
Selenium 34mcg
Niacin 2.7mg

Wheat Bran

Wheat bran is the outer shell of the kernel of wheat and one of nature's richest sources of fiber. The taste is subtle with a touch of sweetness.

benefits

Adding wheat bran to your food is a great way to boost the fiber content of your diet. Research shows that people who eat a diet rich in fiber—including fruits, vegetables, whole grains, nuts and legumes—are less likely to suffer from health problems such as constipation, hemorrhoids, obesity, type 2 diabetes, high blood pressure and cardiovascular disease. An increase in dietary fiber also appears to be helpful in treating these conditions. Wheat bran's fiber is primarily insoluble, the type that promotes good digestion, produces regularity and helps sweep the intestines of potentially toxic contents. Wheat bran is also a good source of essential nutrients, including niacin and other B vitamins, zinc, potassium, magnesium and manganese.

selection and storage

Wheat bran is usually available in the natural foods section or with the cereal products at the supermarket. Keep wheat bran refrigerated in an airtight container to extend its shelf life.

preparation and serving tips

Wheat bran can be added to many foods. Try sprinkling it over hot or cold cereals, yogurt, cottage cheese or applesauce. Mix into ground meat or add it to casseroles as a meat extender. Wheat bran also makes a healthy addition to breads, cookies, muffins or pancakes. Toasting wheat bran gives it an extra nutty flavor and crunchy texture. Because wheat bran is a concentrated source of fiber, add it gradually if your diet has been low in fiber. Be sure to drink plenty of liquids as you add more fiber to your diet.

nutrients per serving:

Wheat Bran
½ cup

Calories 63
Protein 5g
Total Fat 1g
Saturated Fat 0g
Cholesterol 0mg
Carbohydrate 19g
Dietary Fiber 12g
Sodium 0mg
Potassium 345mg
Magnesium 177mg
Iron 3.1mg
Zinc 2.1mg
Niacin 3.9mg
Vitamin B$_6$ 0.4mg

berry bran muffins

2 cups dry bran cereal
1¼ cups fat-free (skim) milk
½ cup packed brown sugar
¼ cup vegetable oil
1 egg, lightly beaten
1 teaspoon vanilla
1¼ cups all-purpose flour
1 tablespoon baking powder
¼ teaspoon salt
1 cup fresh or frozen blueberries (partially thawed if frozen)

1. Preheat oven to 350°F. Line 12 standard (2¾-inch) muffin cups with paper baking cups.

2. Mix cereal and milk in medium bowl; let stand 5 minutes to soften. Add brown sugar, oil, egg and vanilla; beat well. Combine flour, baking powder and salt in large bowl. Stir in cereal mixture just until dry ingredients are moistened. Gently fold in blueberries. Fill prepared muffin cups almost full.

3. Bake 20 to 25 minutes (25 to 30 if using frozen berries) or until toothpick inserted into centers comes out clean. Serve warm.

Makes 12 servings

nutrients per serving:

Calories 172
Calories from Fat 27%
Protein 4g
Carbohydrate 29g
Fiber 4g
Total Fat 5g
Saturated Fat 1g
Cholesterol 18mg
Sodium 287mg

Yogurt

Yogurt has been appreciated for thousands of years as a way to preserve milk. Friendly bacteria turn milk into a creamy, tangy treat that has the health benefits of milk and more.

benefits

Yogurt is made from milk, so it offers as much bone-building calcium as milk does. You can further enhance the benefits by selecting yogurt with added vitamin D. Most yogurt contains live active bacteria cultures. Research suggests yogurt with active cultures may help combat a variety of gastrointestinal problems—such as constipation, diarrhea, lactose intolerance, ulcer, inflammatory bowel disease and possibly colon cancer—by bolstering the body's immune response and rebalancing microorganisms naturally present in the gut.

selection and storage

Always choose yogurt that contains live cultures. To limit fat and calories, choose low-fat or nonfat yogurt and be aware that flavored yogurt can contain surprising amounts of sugar. Check the nutrition label to see what's been added. Better yet, purchase plain yogurt and add your own fresh fruit. Check for a "sell-by" date on the carton; yogurt will keep for up to ten days past that date.

preparation and serving tips

Yogurt makes a great portable lunch or snack. If you don't have access to a refrigerator, freeze the carton overnight, then thaw it in time for lunch. Yogurt also makes a delicious dessert or a wonderful smoothie blended with fresh fruit. Mix yogurt into your cereal instead of milk for breakfast. Yogurt also substitutes beautifully in most recipes that call for high-fat ingredients such as heavy cream or sour cream. And nonfat yogurt makes a healthy base for dips and salad dressings.

nutrients per serving:

Yogurt, plain low-fat 1 cup

Calories 154
Protein 13g
Total Fat 4g
Saturated Fat 2.5g
Cholesterol 15mg
Carbohydrate 17g
Dietary Fiber 0g
Sodium 170mg
Potassium 575mg
Calcium 448mg
Magnesium 42mg
Vitamin A 125 IU
Vitamin B₁₂ 1mcg
Vitamin C 2mg
Vitamin D 2 IU
Folate 27mcg

lemon yogurt pudding with blueberry sauce

1 cup plain fat-free yogurt
Grated peel of ½ lemon
1 tablespoon fresh lemon juice, divided
½ teaspoon vanilla
4 packets sugar substitute
¾ cup fresh blueberries, divided
1½ teaspoons sugar
1 teaspoon cornstarch

1. Line strainer with cheesecloth or coffee filter and place over bowl. Spoon yogurt into lined strainer. Cover with plastic wrap and refrigerate 12 hours or overnight.

2. Discard drained liquid. Whisk thickened yogurt, lemon peel, 1½ teaspoons lemon juice, vanilla and 3 packets sugar substitute in large bowl until smooth. Cover and refrigerate 1 hour.

3. For blueberry sauce, mash half of blueberries with fork. Combine mashed and whole blueberries, remaining 1½ teaspoons lemon juice, sugar and cornstarch in small saucepan; mix well. Cook over medium-high heat 4 minutes or until mixture is thickened. Remove from heat and cool 2 minutes. Stir in remaining 1 packet sugar substitute.

4. Divide yogurt mixture evenly among two small dessert bowls or stemmed glasses. Top with warm blueberry sauce. Serve immediately.

Makes 2 servings

nutrients per serving:

Calories 124
Calories from Fat 3%
Protein 9g
Carbohydrate 22g
Fiber 2g
Total Fat <1g
Saturated Fat <1g
Cholesterol 2mg
Sodium 91mg

Zucchini

Zucchini is everyone's favorite summer squash. It's sweet and delicate enough to enjoy raw and versatile enough to make a tasty addition to stir-fries, casseroles or baked goods.

nutrients per serving:

Zucchini
½ cup cooked

Calories 14
Protein 1g
Total Fat 0g
Saturated Fat 0g
Cholesterol 0mg
Carbohydrate 2g
Dietary Fiber 1g
Sodium 0mg
Potassium 240mg
Calcium 16mg
Iron 0.3mg
Vitamin A 1,005 IU
Vitamin C 12mg
Folate 25mcg

benefits

Its high water content makes zucchini one of the least caloric vegetables in the produce section. And zucchini offers folate, an essential B vitamin that pregnant women need in order to protect their babies from birth defects of the brain and spinal cord. Folate, along with the vitamins A and C, also helps to protect the cells in the heart and throughout the body from damage that can lead to heart disease and cancer. Zucchini's fiber helps to lower blood cholesterol and blood sugar levels, while its potassium content helps to maintain a steady heartbeat and healthy blood pressure.

selection and storage

Zucchini are available year-round in the supermarket, but for a better selection visit a farmers' market. You'll find the standard dark green zucchini as well as yellow varieties, striped ones and even round zucchini the size of a baseball. Smaller squash have a sweeter flavor and better texture. They should be firm and unblemished and feel heavy for their size. Store zucchini in the refrigerator, but plan to use them within a few days.

preparation and serving tips

The mild flavor of zucchini complements other ingredients in a variety of dishes. They are delicious sautéed with tomatoes and onions, and they make a tasty and nutritious addition to vegetable lasagna, marinara sauce and ratatouille. The perfect way to use a larger zucchini is to grate it and bake it into a low-fat cake or quick bread to help keep it moist and tender.

zucchini spice bundt cake

1 package (about 18 ounces) spice or
    carrot cake mix
1 cup water
¾ cup cholesterol-free egg substitute
2 tablespoons canola oil
1 medium zucchini, shredded
3 tablespoons chopped walnuts, toasted*
¾ teaspoon vanilla
¼ cup powdered sugar
1 to 2 teaspoons fat-free (skim) milk

*To toast walnuts, spread in single layer on baking
sheet. Bake in preheated 350°F oven 5 to 7 minutes
or until fragrant and lightly browned.

1. Preheat oven to 325°F. Spray 12-cup bundt
pan with nonstick cooking spray.

2. Combine cake mix, water, egg substitute
and oil in large bowl; mix according to
package directions. Stir in zucchini, walnuts
and vanilla until well blended. Pour into
prepared pan.

3. Bake 40 minutes or until toothpick
inserted near center comes out almost clean.
Cool in pan 10 minutes. Remove to wire rack;
cool completely.

4. Combine powdered sugar and milk in
small bowl; stir until smooth. Drizzle evenly
over cake.   *Makes 18 servings*

nutrients per serving:

Calories 154
Calories from Fat 28%
Protein 2g

Carbohydrate 25g
Fiber <1g
Total Fat 5g
Saturated Fat 1g
Cholesterol 0mg
Sodium 205mg

Glossary

Amino acids: the building blocks of protein. The body needs 20 amino acids to grow, repair itself and fight disease. Of these, 11 can be made by the body, and 9 cannot. These 9 are referred to as "essential" because you must get them from your diet.

Antioxidant: certain vitamins, minerals and enzymes that help protect cells from damage caused by oxidation, which can result from normal body functions as well as from exposure to tobacco smoke, sunlight, radiation and pollution. Antioxidants offer protection against heart disease, cancer, diabetes, eye disease and numerous other health problems.

Beta-carotene: a potent antioxidant found in red, orange and yellow plant foods and in some dark green vegetables. It can be converted to vitamin A in the body.

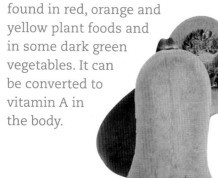

Carbohydrate: one of the three main nutrients in food, providing 4 calories per gram. Complex carbohydrates are the primary supplier of energy in the diet and include nutrient-rich starches like breads, cereals, pasta, potatoes, squash, beans and peas. Sugars are also known as simple carbohydrates and provide calories (and energy) with few nutrients.

Carotenoids: pigments that give produce their red, orange and yellow colors. Over 600 different carotenoids have been identified, some of which are powerful antioxidants, including beta-carotene, lutein and lycopene.

Cholesterol: a waxy substance produced by your liver that is part of every cell in the body. The body uses it to manufacture hormones, bile acid and other essential substances. It is also supplied by animal foods in the diet. Some cholesterol is essential for life, but too much can build up on artery walls and narrow blood vessels. LDL, or "bad," cholesterol molecules deposit cholesterol in blood vessels, where it forms plaque that can lead to heart attack and stroke. HDL, or "good," cholesterol molecules help remove cholesterol from the blood and deliver it to the liver, where it can be eliminated.

Cruciferous vegetables: a family of vegetables, including bok choy, broccoli, brussels sprouts, cabbage, cauliflower, kale, mustard greens and turnips, with cancer- and inflammation-fighting properties. The family is named for its cross-shaped flowers.

Fat: one of the three major nutrients in food, providing 9 calories per gram. Saturated fats, which predominate in butter, stick margarine, meat, poultry skin and whole-fat dairy foods, are solid at room temperature and tend to raise blood cholesterol levels. Unsaturated fats, the dominant fat in vegetable oils, fish, nuts, olives and avocados, are liquid at room temperature and help lower blood cholesterol

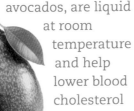

levels when they replace saturated fats in the diet. Unsaturated fats include the monounsaturated fat in olive oil and the polyunsaturated fat in fish, many nuts and seeds, and vegetable oils such as safflower, corn and soybean.

Fiber: the parts of plants that cannot be digested. Insoluble fiber absorbs water and adds bulk to stools, easing elimination, promoting regularity and providing a feeling of fullness after eating. Soluble fiber forms a gel in the digestive tract and slows the rate of digestion, which helps regulate blood sugar levels and prevent the absorption of cholesterol.

Flavonoids: health-protective substances found in the colorful skins of vegetables and fruits and in beverages such as tea, red wine and fruit juices. Their health benefits are similar to those of antioxidants.

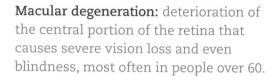

Glucose: the basic form of sugars and carbohydrates found in food. It is transported in the blood, which delivers it to the body's cells to be used for energy. Blood glucose is another name for blood sugar.

Immune function: the body's ability to defend itself against disease and illness.

Insulin: a hormone made by the body that helps the body transfer glucose from the blood into cells, where it can be used to fuel body functions.

Legumes: edible seeds that grow in pods; includes beans, peas, lentils and peanuts.

Macular degeneration: deterioration of the central portion of the retina that causes severe vision loss and even blindness, most often in people over 60.

Metabolic syndrome: a combination of conditions, including high blood pressure, high blood sugar, too much fat around the waist, low HDL ("good") cholesterol and high triglycerides, that tend to occur together and, when they do, increase the risk of diabetes, heart disease and stroke.

Omega-3 fats: a type of unsaturated fat essential for human health that is found in fish, including salmon, tuna and halibut; other seafood, including algae and krill; some plants; and nut oils. These healthy fats play a critical role in brain function, as well as normal growth and development, and they help reduce inflammation that can lead to heart disease, cancer and arthritis.

Osteoporosis: a condition in which the bones become porous and can break easily.

Pectin: a soluble fiber that helps to lower artery-damaging LDL cholesterol. It is found in most plants but is most abundant in apples, cranberries, plums, grapefruits, lemons and oranges.

Plaque: the fatty substance that builds up in blood vessels. It can constrict blood flow and lead to heart attack and stroke.

Protein: one of the three major nutrients in food, providing 4 calories per gram. Protein consists of amino acids, is found in all body tissues, and helps the body grow, repair itself and fight disease. Vegetable sources include beans, nuts and whole grains. Animal sources include fish, poultry and meat. A food provides "complete protein" if it includes all 9 essential amino acids. Animal foods provide complete protein, as do soybeans.

Phytochemicals: another name for phytonutrients.

Phytonutrients: natural substances in plants that help protect the plant from disease. In humans, phytonutrients have numerous health-promoting properties; they function as antioxidants and help rid the body of toxins and prevent inflammation.

Polyphenols: natural chemicals in fruits, vegetables, seeds, legumes and grains that are responsible for much of their color, flavor and aroma. They protect health by functioning as antioxidants and by blocking enzymes that can promote cancer growth.

Triglycerides: the name for fat that travels in your blood, where it is transported to cells and used for energy. High levels of triglycerides can raise your risk of heart disease.

Metric Conversion Chart

VOLUME MEASUREMENTS (dry)

1/8 teaspoon = 0.5 mL
1/4 teaspoon = 1 mL
1/2 teaspoon = 2 mL
3/4 teaspoon = 4 mL
1 teaspoon = 5 mL
1 tablespoon = 15 mL
2 tablespoons = 30 mL
1/4 cup = 60 mL
1/3 cup = 75 mL
1/2 cup = 125 mL
2/3 cup = 150 mL
3/4 cup = 175 mL
1 cup = 250 mL
2 cups = 1 pint = 500 mL
3 cups = 750 mL
4 cups = 1 quart = 1 L

VOLUME MEASUREMENTS (fluid)

1 fluid ounce (2 tablespoons) = 30 mL
4 fluid ounces (1/2 cup) = 125 mL
8 fluid ounces (1 cup) = 250 mL
12 fluid ounces (1 1/2 cups) = 375 mL
16 fluid ounces (2 cups) = 500 mL

WEIGHTS (mass)

1/2 ounce = 15 g
1 ounce = 30 g
3 ounces = 90 g
4 ounces = 120 g
8 ounces = 225 g
10 ounces = 285 g
12 ounces = 360 g
16 ounces = 1 pound = 450 g

DIMENSIONS

1/16 inch = 2 mm
1/8 inch = 3 mm
1/4 inch = 6 mm
1/2 inch = 1.5 cm
3/4 inch = 2 cm
1 inch = 2.5 cm

OVEN TEMPERATURES

250°F = 120°C
275°F = 140°C
300°F = 150°C
325°F = 160°C
350°F = 180°C
375°F = 190°C
400°F = 200°C
425°F = 220°C
450°F = 230°C

BAKING PAN SIZES

Utensil	Size in Inches/Quarts	Metric Volume	Size in Centimeters
Baking or Cake Pan (square or rectangular)	8×8×2	2 L	20×20×5
	9×9×2	2.5 L	23×23×5
	12×8×2	3 L	30×20×5
	13×9×2	3.5 L	33×23×5
Loaf Pan	8×4×3	1.5 L	20×10×7
	9×5×3	2 L	23×13×7
Round Layer Cake Pan	8×1½	1.2 L	20×4
	9×1½	1.5 L	23×4
Pie Plate	8×1¼	750 mL	20×3
	9×1¼	1 L	23×3
Baking Dish or Casserole	1 quart	1 L	—
	1½ quart	1.5 L	—
	2 quart	2 L	—